MODERN DATING

A FIELD GUIDE

From the experts at

ʜhowabout*we*

CHIARA ATIK

Foreword by

**BRIAN SCHECHTER
& AARON SCHILDKROUT**

HARLEQUIN | MELCHER MEDIA

HARLEQUIN®

MELCHER MEDIA

howabout*we*.com

MODERN DATING: A Field Guide

ISBN-13: 978-0-373-89277-8

© 2013 This Life, Inc.

Additional credits appear on page 222 and represent an extension of the copyright page.

Library of Congress Cataloging-in-Publication Data available

www.Harlequin.com

Printed in China
10 9 8 7 6 5 4 3 2 1

To all the women everywhere

taking that final big breath before a first date,

we dedicate this book.

CONTENTS

FOREWORD

O N THE MORNING we launched
HowAboutWe.com, Chiara Atik wrote
an article for the website Guest of a
Guest titled "HowAboutWe.com: A Dating
Site We Might All Actually Use."

The headline captured exactly the spirit
behind HowAboutWe. We wanted to build a
truly modern dating website that was about
having experiences with new people in the
real world. It would be "the offline dating site"
and would be centered around people suggesting "How about we . . . " date ideas. It would be
the first dating site that was natural and . . . not
lame. Chiara—whom we had never met—
understood what we were trying to build: a
dating site we might actually use.

We had the good fortune to meet Chiara
that evening at a happy hour; we knew right
away that, indeed, she did *get it*. She saw in
HowAboutWe a new way of dating that
matched the radically new romantic ethos
and desires of our generation. Chiara herself
was a muse of sorts for this new outlook.

A few months later, Chiara joined the
HowAboutWe team and became a central
voice for our blog, *The Date Report*, chroni-
cling the intricacies of modern dating. She
has borne close witness to the growth of
HowAboutWe (over the past two years, more
than a million people have joined the site) and
has become a thoughtful, delightfully outspo-
ken advocate for our generation's inventive
take on romance.

Last year, the three of us decided together
that it would be amazing if Chiara wrote, as an
expert from HowAboutWe, a comprehensive
field guide to modern dating.

It's a timely project. Not only is our generation staying single longer than any generation in history, we are also doing so in a far
more complex, nuanced, and . . . well . . . *modern* landscape: texting, sexting, longer life
expectancy, unprecedented sexual and economic freedom for women, the INTERNET!,
a dramatic new spirit of individualism and
entrepreneurism, and so on. Modern dating
needs a field guide.

Chiara's basic mission is to free dating from the antiquated notion that being single is a problem to solve. Modern dating isn't merely a means to an end. It's no longer just about the happily-ever-after.

Modern dating is fundamentally about choice. Whom will you be with? How will you meet that person? How will you act? What will you do together? How do you decide what to share and what not to share? These are questions about who you are and what you want. *Modern Dating: A Field Guide* is here not to lay down a set of rules or judgments, but to support you in finding an approach to dating that feels right *for you*.

There is something about Chiara's attitude—judgment-free, intriguingly insightful, independent, and cheering—that gives you, the reader, total permission to figure out the dating life you want.

Chiara eloquently tells us—through stories, interviews, data, lists, graphics, and punchy prose—the story of modern dating. It's about first-date butterflies and figuring out what you really want from a relationship. It's about meeting each other's friends and apartment hunting and going to your friends' weddings and fighting and making up and falling in love. It's an experience worth having.

—BRIAN SCHECHTER *and*
AARON SCHILDKROUT
Co-founders, HowAboutWe.com

Chapter 1

TOTALLY AND COMPLETELY

SINGLE

———

YOU SAY "SINGLE"
LIKE IT'S A BAD THING

T HERE ARE a billion and one reasons why you might be single: Maybe
you just got out of a serious relationship. Maybe you've decided to take a break
from men for a while. Maybe taking a break
from men is the *last* thing you want, and you
can't imagine committing to just one. And of
course, maybe you *do* want a relationship, but
you just aren't in one right now.

Whatever the reason, the point is, you're
single right now, and whether it's by circum-
stance or design, you might as well enjoy it as
best you can. Because being single, at least in
the way women get to be single today, is a lux-
ury our mothers and grandmothers didn't have.

For centuries and centuries, a woman's
lot in life was based on the supposition that
she would get married, and the sooner the
better. In the Middle Ages, a girl would live in
her parents' house until the ripe old age of

seventeen or so, at which point her father
would march her down the aisle and hand her
off to a husband. The next twenty-five years
would be spent getting pregnant, narrowly
escaping death during childbirth, and picking
out new tapestries for the castle great room,
or whatever it was that women did back then.
(Peasant women basically did the same thing,
minus the tapestries and plus a good ten
hours a day of toiling away in the fields with a
baby strapped to their backs.) The only excep-
tions to the rule? Nuns and prostitutes, aka
celibacy and syphilis. So, yes, the Middle Ages
were pretty bleak.

As the centuries went on, things for
women got better, but not by much. Women in
colonial America were finally able to inherit
their husband's property, thus providing
some of the first examples of American
female autonomy. And never-married women

who could scrape together enough money could often manage to buy cottages, where they would lead relatively quiet lives and do their best to avoid anyone suspecting them of being a witch.

With the industrialization of the nineteenth century, single young girls were given the opportunity to leave home and earn a living in mill towns, the very first example of the single life in America. Sure, they lived in all-girl boarding houses, worked an ungodly number of hours, and made very little money. But they were also allowed to sneak into town for the occasional evening's entertainment, one of the *very* few opportunities for young women to meet men unchaperoned. (Unfortunately, birth control at this point was still ages away, so this single life was pretty finite.)

To be a happy single woman, you needed to be rich, and if you weren't born rich, it was very hard to make your own money.

So the single woman continued to unhappily exist until the twentieth century, which is when things suddenly, miraculously took a turn for the better. First, the car was invented, and what's more, women were allowed to drive. Instantly, women had more autonomy: the ability to leave the house, to get to a job, and, best of all, *to meet men unchaperoned.* Is it any wonder that the sexually promiscuous flapper of the 1920s coincided perfectly with the sudden mass popularization of the automobile? Women have *always* been sexual creatures; it was just a matter of getting a moment alone with a guy outside of the damn parlor. Suddenly, women were smoking, drinking, dancing, and having sex: the germination of single life as we know it. But birth

control was still dicey, and women hadn't entered the workforce quite yet, so they still got married ASAP. If a girl was dating a guy she mostly got along with, and they were both of a certain age (say, twenty-four or so), they would probably get married, because that's just what you did. No "I like you, but I need to see what else is out there . . . " exit clause allowed. (If, five years down the road, the two discovered they weren't so compatible after all, well, tough cookies.)

And then, boom! The Sixties happened, and everything exploded. The most important development, of course, was the birth-control pill: that miraculous little thing that you swallow painlessly in the morning to have worry-free sex all month. (Well, relatively.) The other important development was the rise of the "career girl," a woman who entered the workforce not because she had to support her family or help with the war effort, but simply *because she wanted to.* And when a woman got a job, she often got money, and her own apartment, with no one to look after but herself. So naturally women started to realize, *Wait a minute, if I can have sex outside of marriage, and support myself outside of marriage, WHAT is the big rush?* And for the first time in history, there really wasn't a rush, biological or financial, to get married. Was the Sixties single woman free of stigma? Of course not, but it was a start.

Which brings us to today. Women today get to enjoy all the perks of the sexual revolution and feminism, with the added advantage of the fifty or so years over which they've sunk in. Society is *used* to a single woman now. However *you* may feel about your singleness, no

The
EVOLUTION OF DATING

1100

Héloïse d'Argenteuil, a brilliant scholar renowned throughout Europe for her intellect, fell in love with her intellectual equal (and tutor), Peter Abélard, and hooked up with him on the sly. Her family found out; she was sent to become a nun, and he was castrated.

1400

In *The Canterbury Tales*, the Wife of Bath loves sex, but she can have it only within the bounds of matrimony. The solution: She gets married again and again and again....

1300s

Condoms existed in the Middle Ages, but they were made out of pig bladders, tied on, and reused.

1590

In Shakespeare's *A Midsummer Night's Dream*, Hermia refuses to marry her betrothed, Demetrius. She is informed by her father and the Duke Theseus that her other options are lifelong celibacy or the death penalty.

1650s

In colonial America, the law gave parents the right to "dispose of their children in marriage," which gives you a clue as to how romantic things were back then. Marriages were mostly economic arrangements of mutual benefit to the families. Love would (maybe?) develop after the wedding.

1620

Ah, the good old days, when men outnumbered women in America, so much so that "pure and spotless" women from Europe were shipped to Virginia, where they were auctioned off to lonely bachelors for about eighty pounds of tobacco apiece.

1813

Jane Austen published *Pride and Prejudice*, the story of five adolescent sisters stuck together in a house with absolutely nothing to do except hope that a rich man would come into town and fall in love with them. The impossibility of their situation made it a beloved classic for the next two hundred years.

1860s

It's rumored that Queen Victoria instructed her daughter to "lie back and think of England" while performing her "wifely duties." Whether or not this is true, the Victorian era was characterized by its buttoned-up, no-nonsense attitude toward sex.

1750

Finally! A sexual revolution of sorts. Blame the Age of Enlightenment, blame upward mobility, blame "something in the air," but by the middle of the eighteenth century, the number of illegitimate children and pregnant brides soared to unprecedented levels.

1641

Mary Latham, an 18-year-old girl, married a much older man. She had an affair with someone closer to her age, was found out, and was eventually put to death for adultery. How... puritanical.

1849

The California Gold Rush lured a generation of young men west. It would take, on average, forty to sixty days for letters to reach their sweethearts back home. This was called (aptly) "slow courting."

1900

Women were allowed to have multiple "beaus," provided they entertained them in the parlor with their mother, father, siblings, and probably a few cousins around for good measure. A woman could be courted, become engaged to, and eventually marry a man without ever having been in a room alone with him.

1960

The FDA approved the first oral contraceptive.

1950

The end of WWII ushered in a new era of "going steady": long-term, exclusive relationships that often included sex.

1930s

Young people in the Thirties would double-date at movies, ice cream parlors, and Big Band concerts. Because dating was so casual (and an important sign of popularity), a girl wouldn't think twice about having multiple dates a week. Fun!

1920

With the prevalence of cars, suddenly women were whisked away from their parlors and out to dance halls, speakeasys, and jazz clubs, where they participated in lascivious activities such as the newly coined "necking."

1945

WWII. With people so uncertain about their future, the average age for getting married dropped. By 1949, 47 percent of brides were nineteen. (Hello, baby boom!)

1953

The first issue of *Playboy* was published. Never again would a man go into a relationship without knowing what a woman's naked body looks like.

1981

The AIDS virus was identified, swiftly bringing an end to the sexual freedom of the Seventies.

1993

The first dating site, Match.com, was started.

1969

Woodstock. Hippies advocated "free love," squares became increasingly comfortable with the idea of sex outside of marriage, and STD rates ran rampant.

2004

Facebook was born, ushering in the era of Internet stalking. Everyone knows way too much about whom they've dated in the past and whom they might date in the future.

1970

The Mary Tyler Moore Show aired, the first television show about an adult woman living on her own in the city.

1998

In Nora Ephron's *You've Got Mail*, Meg Ryan and Tom Hanks amazed the world by showing that you can fall in love via the Internet.

1962

Helen Gurley Brown published *Sex and the Single Girl*, a book that radically advocated casual sex.

1983

The first cell phones were sold commercially, giving him NO EXCUSE NOT TO CALL.

2010

HowAboutWe.com launched, singlehandedly solving all the problems of modern dating (or at least, how to deal with your love life online).

one is going to give you a dirty look for buying condoms, or signing a lease on your own, or booking a vacation for one.

All the things that you enjoy or appreciate about being single—absolute control over the DVR, coming and going whenever you please, making decisions based on your desires alone, the excitement of going out and meeting new people, the lack of responsibility for just a *little* while longer—these are all things that your grandmother probably didn't have the opportunity to choose for herself.

And as you no doubt know, being single doesn't mean being lonely. You may joke about becoming a cat lady, but you're probably not spending your Saturday nights knitting. You've got friends, you've got interests, you've got hobbies, and you have every opportunity to pursue them. Is being single amazing *all* the time? Definitely not. But then again, as your coupled-up friends can tell you, neither is being in a relationship.

This is not to say that it's bad to want to *not* be single. It's okay to want a boyfriend, to want to get married, and to want it to happen sooner rather than later. And maybe every once in a while, you do get a little lonely. That's normal. You don't have to want to be single forever. But as long as you are, you might as well enjoy it while you can. Someday you might stop being single, and if all goes well, who knows? You might never have the opportunity to be on your own again.

So, seriously: Live it up! Your great-grandmothers would want you to.

MARRIED PEOPLE IN THE U.S. (18+):

1960

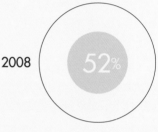

2008

According to the Pew Research Center, in 1960, 72% of Americans 18+ were married (85%, if divorced, separated, and widowed individuals are included). By 2008, those figures had declined to 52% and 73%. In other words,

the percentage of people who had never married grew from 15% to 27%.

FIFTEEN THINGS TO ENJOY WHILE YOU'RE SINGLE

---

1. Sleeping Diagonally on the Bed
Can we momentarily let go of the illusion that sharing a bed with someone is actually comfortable? It's tolerable at best. But having an entire bed to yourself is *great*.

2. Wild Nights!
It's pretty nice to be able to go out and stay out as long as you want without having to worry about whether your significant other is tired, or his feet hurt, or that you said you'd call, or that he's just ready to go home and have sex now.

And if, at midnight, a friend calls and invites you to come out, you can just go.

And if, at 2 a.m., you meet someone you like, you can just kiss him, or go home with him, or just get his number.

And if, at 4 a.m., you feel like getting a slice of pizza, or a whole pizza, or a whole pizza with extra-garlicky garlic knots, you can, no problem. Who's going to care?

3. Quiet Weekends!
Conversely, if you want to spend an entire weekend ensconced in your room and watch seasons one to four of *The West Wing*, and order delivery, and sleep all afternoon, and wear your rattiest sweatpants, and stalk people on Facebook 'cause you're just in that kind of mood, you can. You can ignore all phone calls and basically disappear from the world without feeling too neglectful or guilty.

4. The Opportunity to Check Out All Those "What-Ifs"
A random person you meet at a party, an acquaintance you've had a crush on forever, maybe even a co-worker: When you're single, you can pursue these "what-ifs" and see where they lead. More often than not, these little sparks of romance turn out to be nothing, but at least when you're single, the not knowing won't drive you crazy.

5. Spending Your Money on What You Want
No need to justify that $300 dress; no need to put money aside for *his* friend's wedding or Christmas presents for *his* family.

6. Not Having to Hang Out with Anyone Else's Friends
You have your own friends, and it's hard enough to find time to hang out with them. So it's pretty nice not to have to waste a perfectly good Friday night at a bar with his buddies (who aren't half as cool as yours).

7. Guiltless Flirting
Flirting is one of life's simplest pleasures and easiest confidence-boosters. Maintaining eye

contact just a beat longer than normal, engaging in a little repartee, touching someone's arm, sending a few playful texts that may or may not lead anywhere. It all puts an extra spring in your step, doesn't it?

8. You Have the Best Stories
Your crazy, roller-coaster dating stories make you the most popular person at brunch. Dating and hookup stories may not end in "happily ever after," but they're almost always entertaining.

9. Big Decisions Are Yours and Yours Alone to Make . . .
If something happens in your life—a job opportunity, a lifestyle change, a sudden trip, a need for something new—you don't have to consult anyone else. You don't have to consider anyone else. Your decisions affect you and you alone, so you never have to compromise or turn down an opportunity for someone else.

10. . . . And So Is the Remote Control
You're going to watch that *Toddlers & Tiaras* marathon in its entirety, and ain't nobody going to stop you.

11. Eat Whatever, Whenever You Want
Something about being in a relationship seems to put a lot of pressure on meals. Whereas a single person can just pour herself a bowl of cereal for dinner, a couple will more often than not feel the need to "go get food" or put together an entire meal. You can enjoy eating without feeling the pressure of making dinner a big production.

12. You Can Have Sex with Anyone If You Want To
People in relationships can't.

13. Privacy
People always say that one of the pleasures of being in a relationship is finding someone with whom you can always be yourself, and do anything in front of. But just for the moment, enjoy the fact that you don't ever have to see or hear anyone clipping their toenails, and vice versa.

14. Spontaneity
Couples have to be spontaneous *together*. Single people can decide on last-minute trips, after-work plans, or impromptu weekend activities without checking with anyone first.

15. First Dates
First dates are scary, and they don't always turn out well, but they're always, always laced with possibility. Every first date you go on could be your last for a while, really, so enjoy the excitement, the butterflies, the hope, and the *unknown*. It's something you'll miss once you're happily settled.

I'VE NEVER HAD A BOYFRIEND

"I'm turning twenty-six pretty soon, and I've never had a boyfriend, nor have I ever dated short-term or casually. I've liked guys, and a couple have even liked me, but they haven't really matched up. The ones that have liked me are both longer-term guy friends who became interested only after several months of knowing me. Is that bad/weird?"

—LARISSA, 25, MINNEAPOLIS

"Bad/weird?" Maybe just unusual/not great. But don't worry about the past too much, and start looking ahead: Do you want to get more experience under your belt in the romance department? If you've liked guys and guys have liked you, then there's literally nothing keeping you from going out and finding someone to date short-term or casually *tomorrow.*

That's the danger about being single for a really long time: not that it's weird or bad per se, but that it can create sort of a mental roadblock in your own mind. We become so used to being alone that we can't even imagine a scenario where we're not. We have no idea how to take those simple steps from platonic to romantic—single is normal, single is status quo, and romantic is not.

If you want a boyfriend, you can get one, but it's definitely going to mean pushing yourself out of your comfort zone. (Being single is comfortable, if nothing else.) Go up and talk to people at parties. Sign up for an online dating site and force yourself to go on at least four dates—don't just go on one mediocre date and then give up. If the guys who have liked you in the past did so after several months of knowing you, it suggests that you are slow to open up to people. Force yourself to be friendlier and flirtier to guys when you meet them. What to you might feel overly forward is probably pretty tame.

You might be telling yourself that you're waiting for the right guy to come along. But what you're risking is not knowing how to get his attention when he does come along. Don't lock yourself up in an ivory tower—kiss a guy, have a fling, date someone for a while, and get comfortable with the idea of romance.

And then, if after all that you find you prefer being single to the effort of dating, then by all means become a confirmed bachelorette. But at least at that point, you'll know you're making an informed decision rather than just settling.

NOT THAT IT'S ANYONE'S BUSINESS, BUT...

—————

EVERYONE KNOWS it's not polite to ask a woman her age or her weight. Unfortunately, asking someone why she doesn't have a boyfriend still seems to be allowed. (Personally, I'd way rather tell someone my age and/or weight than have to explain to someone why I happen to be single at that particular moment.) The worst is when people ask by way of paying you a compliment ("Why doesn't a pretty/nice girl like you have a boyfriend?"), as if all your fabulous traits are wasted on you and you alone.

The thing is, it is absolutely no one's *business* why you're single. Not your great aunt's, not your ex-boyfriend's, not the nosy cab driver's or the inappropriate co-worker's. As we've said, there are myriad reasons why you could be single at any given moment, and they're all personal. So the next time someone asks you why you don't have a boyfriend, you are perfectly within your rights to say, "That couldn't *possibly* be less of your business." Except with more expletives.

Of course, it's hard to actually tell people to eff off when you're face-to-face, and they probably are just "politely" inquiring. So what are some things you can actually say when someone asks you why you're (still) single?

If you're really uncomfortable with the question, the best thing you can do is keep your answer short, succinct, and conclusive. Then *immediately* follow it up with a question that swiftly changes the topic.

At a loss as to what to say? Try one of these strategies:

❄ **Deflect the question with a joke.**
  • *I was born this way.*
  • *I didn't realize there was a cutoff age!*
  • *I have yet to meet my match in wit, brains, and beauty.*
  • *Why are you still married?*

❄ **Keep your response honest and simple.**
  • *Because I want to be.*
  • *Because I have too much going on right now to have a relationship.*
  • *I haven't met the right person.*
  • *I just don't think I'm ready to settle down yet.*

❄ **And remember, you can always add:**
  • *Why, do you know someone?*

From the Trenches

THOUGHTS ON SINGLEHOOD

If you subsisted solely on a cultural diet of romantic comedies, you could be forgiven for thinking that a period of singlehood is one of the worst things to happen to a woman. (Cue the shots of a girl in her prime, wearing sweats and crying into her tub of ice cream.) In reality, many women have a much more positive take on being single.

"I had a conversation with my dad—we were at a wedding—and he said, 'I just don't want you to be alone when you're thirty.' And I said to him, 'I appreciate your concern, but if I'm alone at thirty, I'm okay with that. I don't have a timer that's ticking.' I guess I'm not really that worried about it."

—KATHLEEN, 26, BOSTON

"I love driving home from work and thinking, *I can make myself a steak and listen to Lauryn Hill, and answer to no one.*"

—MALLORY, 25, SAN FRANCISCO

"If you have a group of single girlfriends, it's a blast. Everywhere you go, you have the potential to meet someone—not that you're looking, but it could happen. The world is open."

—ROSE, 23, CHICAGO

"I was in a relationship for half of my twenties and then became single again in my early thirties. It took that change for me to realize how much self-discovery I missed out on then, and I've grown so much just in my short time being single. I've focused on new and old passions and really have been having a blast. I love the feeling of freedom that singledom gives me and, frankly, don't want to give it up anytime soon."

—JORDAN, 33, BROOKLYN

"I love being single. I get to make the social plans that I want, instead of having to factor in a partner's agenda, and I can focus on career and life decisions that most fulfill me."

—ANNIE, 32, NEW YORK CITY

FRIENDSHIP

and

DATING

WHEN YOU'RE single and living out on your own, your friends become like a second family to you. They're the ones who meet you for breakfast after a hookup, come over with pizza on Sunday nights, throw you birthday parties, give you a ride to the airport, comfort you during a breakup, keep spare keys to your apartment in case of emergency, celebrate your promotion, tell you that you weren't that drunk last night even though you totally were, analyze all the texts he sends you, approve your outfits before a date, accompany you to boring work events, bring you medicine when you're sick, unflinchingly listen to your weird and embarrassing sex questions, confirm that his new girlfriend is not nearly as cute as you are, GChat you all day at work, and hold your hand through life's best and worst moments. By the time a woman is thirty-six, there's a chance she'll have lived with her best friends for just as long as she lived with her parents as a child. Friends will outlast a good portion of your romantic relationships. In other words, maintaining a good relationship with your friends, through thick and thin, through single and not single, is a big deal.

YOUR FRIENDS KNOW WHY YOU'RE SINGLE

HERE IS something to think about: Your friends know why you're single. Yep! They totally do.

They've known you forever. They've seen you interact with countless men. They've heard all your relationship stories. And let's face it, when it comes to your love life, they're definitely more objective than you are. Maybe they've noticed your flirting style comes off as a bit mean. Maybe you never give the nice guys a chance. Maybe (and they mean this in the *nicest* possible way) you can be a little bit of a demanding, high-maintenance girlfriend? You might be completely at a loss as to why you don't have a boyfriend right now, but your friends probably have a pretty good idea.

Now, whether or not you want them to *tell* you your thing is a different story.

Are you perfectly happy with your relationship status? Are you super-sensitive and prone to reacting badly when faced with constructive criticism? Are you already pretty neurotic about this stuff and don't need yet another thing to obsess over? Then do not beg or cajole your friends into telling you what your "thing" is. It's really more trouble than it's worth.

On the other hand . . .

If you're single, and you don't want to be; if you feel like you fall into the same dating patterns and you don't quite know why; if the guys you like never, *ever* seem to like you back and you're at the end of your rope . . . you might want to consider asking a friend for an honest conversation.

Of course, it's a dangerous game, asking someone to be brutally honest with you. If you decide to do it, make sure it's a friend you absolutely trust (and maybe someone who will cushion the blow a bit?). Make sure she knows that this is *not* an opportunity to go through a laundry list of things she thinks are wrong with you. Just, you know, the main things. The ones that are scaring the guys away.

And remember! You *asked* your friend to tell you! So you aren't allowed to get upset or defensive. If you don't like what you hear, you are allowed to completely ignore it. But maybe, just maybe, there's a *grain* of truth for you to consider, somewhere in there.

HOW TO WING FOR OTHER WOMEN

WANT TO learn a skill that will make you beloved among your girlfriends and that will entertain you long after you cease to be single? Learn how to be a great wingwoman. It's not brain surgery, no, but it does take a certain finesse. Picking out a guy for your friend, breaking the ice, then seamlessly taking yourself out of the picture will leave you feeling downright beatific. And, not that your reasons for winging would be anything other than altruistic, but the better you wing for your friend, the more likely she is to do it for you. Here are ten things to keep in mind:

1. Make sure you and your partner/protégé have different taste.

The perfect wing relationship between two single women is one in which the parties have completely opposite taste in men. If one girl likes mountain men and the other likes preps? Perfect! If both parties like broody hipsters, then you're forced to go through a really awkward back-and-forth of "Oh . . . you can have him . . . "/"No, no, you go ahead . . . "

2. Give good pep talks.

Obviously you know how awesome and funny and cool your friend is, but there's a chance she's not so sure about it when faced with the daunting task of talking to/approaching men. So pep her up! You are her coach, and she is going to go out there and WIN THE GAME of

meeting someone tonight! The more confident you can get her to feel about herself right off the bat, the less work you'll have to do later in the night.

3. Initiate contact with the guy your friend likes.

People are usually more shy when it comes to starting a conversation with someone they're interested in, so check your pride at the door and break the ice so she doesn't have to. Anything to get the conversation started, from "What's the score?" to "Will you pass the napkins?" will do!

4. Talk up your friend, but not too obviously.

BAD:
Cute Guy: Oh, I love this song!
You: Really? OMG! Melissa ALSO loves music!
GOOD:
Cute Guy: Oh, I love this song!
You: Hey, Melissa, isn't this by that band you're always trying to get me to listen to?

5. Don't engage with him too much.

You want your friend to be the one who stands out, so remember, your only job is to facilitate the beginning of a conversation and then *get out of there*. If you talk to him too long, he might end up preferring you. You'll feel awkward, and your friend will feel horrible. Avoid at all costs.

6. **Take bathroom breaks early and often.**
You wanna see if this thing is gonna sink or float as soon as possible, so take a bathroom break and give the conversation a chance to breathe without you. If they're still talking when you get back, and if neither looks especially relieved upon your return, you're good; if not, help her move on to the next guy.

7. **Take one for the team.**
So the guy has an annoying/not cute/chatty friend. You know what I'm gonna say, don't you? Step up to the plate and take one for the team. Be friendly and keep him occupied while giving your friend a chance to talk to her quarry uninterrupted.

8. **Know when to bow out.**
The mark of a truly excellent wingwoman is knowing when to bow out. As soon as you see that the conversation is tripping along successfully without your help (and you've tested this with at least two bathroom breaks), stretch your arms, yawn, and announce that you're calling it a night. Be VERY decisive in your language ("I'm gonna head home . . .

have a good night, guys!") so your friend won't be put in the position of having to decide whether or not to leave with you. (If you say, "Sooo . . . I think I'm gonna take off . . . Melissa, are you gonna stay?" and Melissa is shy, it might be sort of awkward for her to have to say, "Uh, I guess . . . I dunno . . . .")

9. **DO NOT LEAVE UNLESS SHE IS OKAY.**
The absolutely most important thing you can do as a wingwoman, friend, and all-around decent human being is look out for your friend. If you think the guy is sketchy, or if you're worried that she's had too much to drink, stay and look out for her. Make sure she's making smart choices.

10. **A wingwoman's job is never over.**
A good wingwoman will be easily reached for text-message updates, and available for brunch or coffee the next day to discuss the entire thing, going over every little detail. Because the day will come when you'll want someone to eagerly discuss the tiniest details of a night with you, too.

You gotta talk to the friend. The friend could look like Shrek, but you still talk to him."

—Briana, 25, Chicago

WHEN YOUR FRIENDS GET BOYFRIENDS

WHILE WE'RE on the subject of being single, let's talk about what happens when your best friend, your wingwoman, your single partner in crime, gets a boyfriend. It kind of secretly sucks, right?

Here's what usually happens: A friend will say something like, "I met a guy last night, and he wants to hang out this weekend!" You'll dutifully plaster a smile on your face and ask her the appropriate questions ("Sooo, how'd you meet him? What's he like?"), all the while fending off a feeling of impending panic and loneliness, because, well, another one bites the dust.

It's not *jealousy* that's the issue. It's the sad sense of inevitable abandonment from a friend. Even though she'll always be there for you (she insists), it's just not quite the same. (There's also that little part of you that is thinking, *Why is it so easy for her??? Why do they like her, not me??? WHAT IS WRONG WITH ME?!*) Her "honeymoon" stage with him can feel a little bit like a mourning stage to you.

When you're single, fellow single ladies can feel like a lifeboat. They're the ones who are always up for spontaneous nights out; the ones who will engage in self-deprecating banter about spinsterhood; the ones you can freely text on a random night because you're fairly sure that they, like you, are sitting around their apartment watching TV. When you get into a relationship, the dynamics, understandably, shift. That's okay. That's how it *should* work.

It's just that it can be a little sad for the single person who's getting, ever-so-slightly, ever-so-slowly, pushed aside.

But.

It's how the world works. And if you're not a horrible person, then it's impossible not to smile when you see your friends incandescently, undeniably *happy*. That's how people act when they're in love, and it's infectious, even to the most bitter of singletons.

Of course, the answer is for you to go on dates. Because, let's face it, it's better to join the Happily Coupled than to wish your friends single again.

But in the meantime . . . make sure you always have *some* friends who remain unattached. A single girl needs 'em.

EVERYTHING YOU COULD POSSIBLY NEED TO KNOW ABOUT FRIENDS WITH BENEFITS

U NLESS YOU'RE living in some weird all-female city that I've somehow managed to never hear of, not all your friends will be women. Probably you'll have guy friends, too, who are great for serving as plus-ones when you need them, giving you the male perspective on your dating life, desperately trying to get you to see the genius in *Blade Runner*, and occasionally helping you lug home an air-conditioning unit. However, they are not good for sleeping with. Do not sleep with your guy friends.

You know that Friends with Benefits never works, right? Of course you know that. You've no doubt heard someone, at some point, authoritatively claim that there's no way two people can have sex and still maintain a friendship.

And everyone is right, of course. It's incredibly hard to maintain a nice, even friendship with someone while also sharing something as intimate as sex—*especially* for women.

By starting a Frenz with Benz relationship (does the nickname make you less inclined to do it?), you're risking your friendship and your sanity. But whatever. You know this, but you might just go ahead and try it anyway.

Fine. Fine! Just keep the following things in mind, okay?

❊ **Do not pick your best friend.**
That guy friend who's like your brother, whom you've been friends with for years, who has seen you through countless breakups and has selflessly helped you move from at least two apartments? Oh my God, *do not sleep with him*. No! He's much too valuable, and the risk of hurting him (or yourself!) is much too great. Instead, choose someone who's on the periphery of your friendship group but not an integral member. Way less awkward when things eventually fizzle out.

❊ **Do not pick the guy you're secretly in love with.**
If you *like* him, tell him. Don't let him use you for sex under the misconception that you aren't interested in any sort of commitment or relationship with him.

❊ **No one is Frenz with Benz forever.**
You are *not* going to be Friends with Benefits with this person forever, or if you are, you should really consider upgrading him to at least "boyfriend" level. Friends with Benefits situations tend to come to a natural end when one of you gets a significant other, or moves away, or simply gets bored with the arrangement. You should both be very aware of this from the get-go to avoid hurt feelings later.

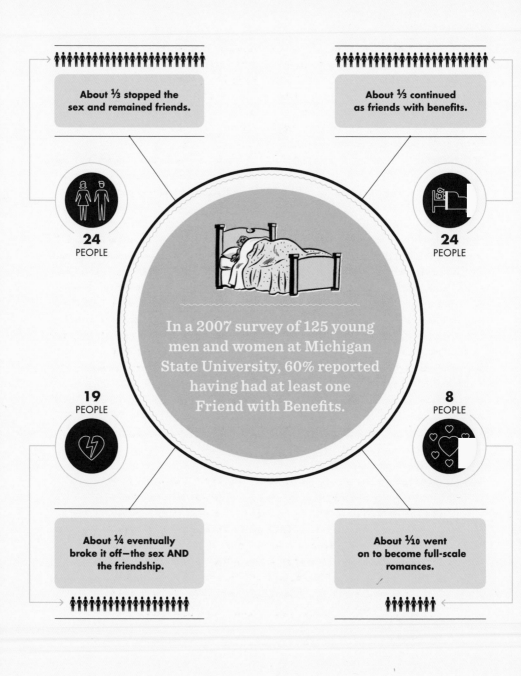

About ⅓ stopped the sex and remained friends.

24 PEOPLE

About ⅓ continued as friends with benefits.

24 PEOPLE

In a 2007 survey of 125 young men and women at Michigan State University, 60% reported having had at least one Friend with Benefits.

19 PEOPLE

8 PEOPLE

About ¼ eventually broke it off—the sex AND the friendship.

About ¹⁄₁₀ went on to become full-scale romances.

✳ If it's weird for you to talk about the other people you're dating, you shouldn't be FWB.

Doubly so if it's weird for you to hear *him* talk about his dating life. Being able to openly discuss the other people you're seeing (if any) is what differentiates Friends with Benefits from just being, like, lovers.

✳ It's Friends with Benefits. Not just Benefits.

Obviously, there's nothing wrong with having a hookup buddy, but Friends with Benefits implies some sort of friendship outside the bedroom. If you have any interest in maintaining this friendship after the benefits stop, be sure to spend platonic time together, alone or in a group, just like you always have.

✳ Avoid at all costs:

Set schedules, seeing each other five nights a week, getting annoyed at each other if one or the other doesn't call or text, any sort of unplatonic affection outside of the bedroom, any sort of "date" scenarios, telling other people you're sleeping together, prolonged cuddling, Valentine's Day.

If you start to feel jealous, or sense that he is; if you find yourself uninterested in anyone else; if you start keeping your nights free so that you can hook up with him: Please, for the love of God, check yourself before you wreck yourself. Are you falling for him? If so, you need to stop hooking up with him *immediately* and have a serious conversation! If at any point the two of you aren't on even ground, it's best to discontinue, if not the friendship then at least the benefits. Stop wasting time and energy having sex with this guy, and use it instead to find a relationship (all benefits included).

"OH, SHIT, IS THIS A DATE?"

Finding out that, surprise! this guy thinks you're on a date! is the worst, but it's pretty easy to make it clear that you aren't interested in that way. Inviting a friend (or even suggesting that you see what so-and-so is up to) is a great way to defuse romantic tension. Make sure to pay for yourself, and drop the friend card as often as possible. ("I totally just needed some low-key friend time.") If he's still not getting the hint, just be blunt. "Hey, I'm having a great time, but I want to make sure I'm not giving the wrong impression." It will be awkward for about three minutes, but then you guys can breathe easy and enjoy the rest of the hangout with no romantic tension.

Can You Be
FRIENDS WITH BENEFITS?

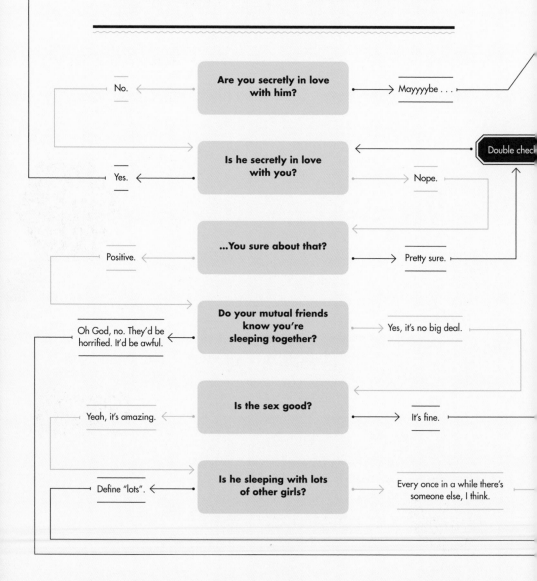

Are you secretly in love with him?

No. → Mayyyybe . . .

Is he secretly in love with you?

Yes. ← Nope.

Double check

...You sure about that?

Positive. ← Pretty sure.

Do your mutual friends know you're sleeping together?

Oh God, no. They'd be horrified. It'd be awful. ← Yes, it's no big deal.

Is the sex good?

Yeah, it's amazing. ← It's fine.

Is he sleeping with lots of other girls?

Define "lots". ← Every once in a while there's someone else, I think.

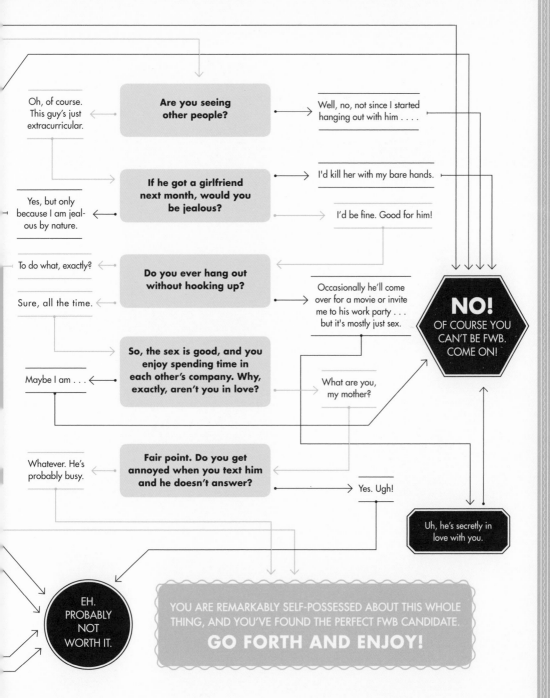

Oh, of course. This guy's just extracurricular.

Are you seeing other people?

Well, no, not since I started hanging out with him . . . .

Yes, but only because I am jealous by nature.

If he got a girlfriend next month, would you be jealous?

I'd kill her with my bare hands.

I'd be fine. Good for him!

To do what, exactly?

Do you ever hang out without hooking up?

Sure, all the time.

Occasionally he'll come over for a movie or invite me to his work party . . . but it's mostly just sex.

NO!
OF COURSE YOU CAN'T BE FWB. COME ON!

So, the sex is good, and you enjoy spending time in each other's company. Why, exactly, aren't you in love?

Maybe I am . . .

What are you, my mother?

Whatever. He's probably busy.

Fair point. Do you get annoyed when you text him and he doesn't answer?

Yes. Ugh!

Uh, he's secretly in love with you.

EH. PROBABLY NOT WORTH IT.

YOU ARE REMARKABLY SELF-POSSESSED ABOUT THIS WHOLE THING, AND YOU'VE FOUND THE PERFECT FWB CANDIDATE.
GO FORTH AND ENJOY!

HOW TO AVOID THE FRIEND ZONE

T HE UNHAPPY inverse of Friends With Benefits is, of course, the Friend Zone. If all of your relationships constantly sway toward the platonic rather than the romantic, then, sorry to say it, it's probably because of something you're doing. Luckily, it is possible to get out of the Friend Zone and stay out for good. It takes a bit of bravery, and just the right amount of physical contact. Some tips:

✳ Establish a flirtatious relationship.

When you meet someone you might be interested in, time is of the essence in terms of establishing whether your relationship will be platonic or romantic. For shy people, the natural tendency is to slowly get to know the other person, even if their attraction is instant. But this is how people get stuck in the Friend Zone: They wait too long, then get to the point where any possible chemistry or attraction has (d)evolved into a comfortable, platonic friendship. (Not that romance can't develop from friendship—but in your case, it hasn't.)

If you think you like someone, make sure your interactions are *flirty* and not friendly. If you find there's no chemistry, it's easy to develop a friendship from there. But turning friendship into romance is much harder.

✳ Don't be too subtle.

It might be painfully obvious to you that you have an enormous crush on someone in your friend group, but trust me: There's a good chance he has no idea. People who frequently get stuck in the Friend Zone are often extremely subtle flirters—unfortunately, eye contact and "a good connection" do not a flirtatious exchange make.

Odds are you're not coming on strongly enough (or at all). If you like someone, let him know you like him! It's worth risking potential rejection or embarrassment. You'll never get the romantic attention you want if you don't send out the signals.

✳ Don't act goofy/self-deprecating.

If you take one thing away from this section, let it be this: Everyone wants goofy friends. They just don't want to sleep with them. I know, it's tough if your natural inclination upon meeting new people is to act goofy and funny so you'll endear yourself to everyone. It totally works—for friendships. Although humor is attractive, constantly making disparaging jokes about yourself or acting like the class clown does not make people think *I have* got *to get this person into bed, and fast.*

Goofy is lovely, funny is charming. So save those qualities for after you've landed a date. When you're first meeting someone, focus instead on friendliness and allure.

❄ **Don't be too available.**
A surefire way to land yourself permanently in the Friend Zone is to be completely available to the other person, with your emotions and your time. Soon you're the one he's texting when he's bored, or inviting out when he has no other plans. You'll feel like you're getting somewhere with this person and may think that if you just continue platonically dating, one of these days he'll look at you across the table and suddenly realize that he's been in love with you this whole time.

Except it very rarely works that way. In truth, he's probably just biding his time with sweet, comfortable you, while thinking of that other girl who is slightly unattainable.

Bottom line: If you like someone, give him the option of dating you, or don't spend too much one-on-one time with him at all. He'll be forced to consider you in a romantic light, and if he turns you down, trust me: It's so much better than being helplessly strung along.

> **Whoever I end up with has to be more interesting than the book I was going to read. I want someone who's going to rock my world a little bit."**
>
> —Jen, 28, New York City

ON WILD OATS,

and

HOW TO SOW THEM

REMEMBER WHEN "sowing one's wild oats" was an idiom that described only men? The term is based around the proclivity of men to experiment sexually before resigning themselves to marriage and (at least nominal) monogamy.

Well, guess what! Having sex with just one person till the end of time (or even just an extended period!) doesn't sound especially thrilling to women, either! Sure, if you met the right person, you'd probably forswear all others. But that hasn't happened yet.

Being single is not akin to taking a vow of celibacy, and these days, women feel the exact same need as men to experiment sexually or at least build up a respectable portfolio of experience. Saving yourself for marriage is all fine and dandy, but so is saving yourself for after dinner at the latest. You're single. You're an adult. You're allowed to do exactly what you want.

It's pretty much a given that when you start dating someone, you'll have sex. When you're not dating anyone or even particularly *looking* to date anyone, that's when the one-night stand comes in.

One-night stands have gotten a bad rap over the years. People have erroneously stated that they make women look easy, when we all know the complicit men were at least ten times easier. In reality, casual sex is a completely harmless way to relieve a sexual craving—as long as you're careful, as long as you're safe, and as long as you have the right expectations.

This is not to say that casual sex is for everyone. You shouldn't feel pressure to be having sex, any more than you should feel pressure to be abstaining from it. The point is, it's your sex life, and you can do with it as you will. (Isn't the twenty-first century great?)

WILL YOU REGRET YOUR ONE-NIGHT STAND?

☒ *Five Signs You Won't*

☐ 1. You don't care if he spends the night afterward: You're in it for the sex; you can take or leave the cuddling.

☐ 2. You wouldn't be ashamed to tell your best friend you slept with this person.

☐ 3. You're really attracted to him, but he's not necessarily the type of guy you'd date. Perfect for something casual!

☐ 4. You're confident enough with your sexuality to be able to enjoy sex the first time with someone.

☐ 5. You're sleeping with him because YOU. Really WANT. To have sex with him. Like, you really, *really*, want to. (Not because you feel like you *should*, or because you owe it to him, or anything.)

☑ *Five Signs You Will*

☐ 1. You're using sex as a way to feel validated and good about yourself.

☐ 2. You think sex with this person might be more meaningful to you than it is to him, or that it's a way to get him to like you.

☐ 3. It's with someone whom, for whatever reason, you *know* you really shouldn't sleep with.

☐ 4. You would never, ever have sex with him sober.

☐ 5. Neither of you has a condom.

SUREFIRE WAYS TO GO HOME WITH SOMEONE

THERE IS A definite upside to being a woman looking for a one-night stand: It's incredibly easy to go home with someone. Maybe not, like, your *dream* guy. But if all you're looking for is a casual hookup (to scratch a biological itch, to keep in practice, or even just to remind yourself that you can), finding someone willing to roll around in the sheets with you is a piece of cake. (Guys are always complaining about how easy girls have it in this respect.)

So let's imagine you're at a party, you've been flirting with the same guy all night, and you definitely want to hook up with him. All you have to say in order to get him to go home with you is some variation of *"I want to have sex with you. Let's go back to my apartment."* Swear to God, this works. And don't worry about sounding slutty: We're all adults here. (Maybe don't go up to complete *strangers* and try this line, though.)

If this approach is a little too direct for your taste (understandable!), you can suggest something slightly more subtle. He'll get the hint, and you won't have to feel like a sexual predator. Keep in mind that you both know what's really being offered here, so no need to

come up with a fake excuse to lure him over. My friend Kevin, twenty-six, from New York, had been talking to a girl at a bar for a few hours when she said to him: "Well, we can stay here, or we can have a couple of drinks on my roof and I can have you on the subway by 11:30." It was the perfect line: Mentioning the subway made it seem like a casual enough invitation, though of course by the time 11:30 rolled around, Kevin had no intention of going home. (He *always* talks about this line, by the way: A girl inviting a guy over for sex is something guys never forget.)

If that's still too forward, remember that making out can be a great euphemism for all kinds of things while keeping the tone fairly light and innocent. Kate, twenty-nine, from New York, has a line she swears by. "My friend thought it up, and I stole it from her 'cause it's *so* good," she says. The line? "It's getting late. I think we should start making out now." Works every time.

If you're really eager to hook up with someone—anyone!—it sometimes helps to be the last person at the bar or party, simply because, at a certain time of night, people just start pairing up. Not that you have to resort to whoever's left, by any means (or that whoever's left is "resorting" to you!). But sometimes you just need to get laid, and opportunities seem to have a way of opening up when it's 2 a.m. or last call.

Truthfully, there's no need to worry too much about "lines" or strategy when it comes to hookups. When you're there and in the moment, things may come out of your mouth that sound so stupid. *Cheesy*, cringe-worthy things that completely work because you're into him and he's into you and maybe you've both had a good bit of alcohol. The most surefire way to go home with someone is to be bold, possibly way bolder than you'd normally be comfortable with. Make eye contact, be friendly, have open body language, and, if necessary, take matters into your own hands. If you're just looking to sow some oats, what do you have to lose?

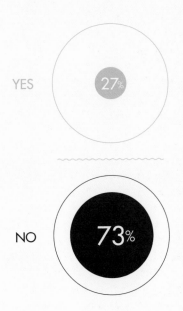

WE ASKED DATERS: HAVE YOU EVER HAD A ONE-NIGHT STAND THAT TURNED INTO A STABLE RELATIONSHIP?

YES 27%

NO 73%

IS SHE INTO WOMEN? A LITMUS TEST

1. Eye Contact

Across the board, women seem to agree that eye contact is the easiest way to tell if another woman is interested in you. It's all in the length of the stare—and the intensity. If you make eye contact with another woman from across the room, does she acknowledge your gaze and then look away? That's inconclusive. But does she hold eye contact with you for at least one Mississippi longer than necessary, hold it for longer than ordinary eye-contact etiquette mandates? That can be a telltale sign. Human beings don't tend to maintain voluntary eye contact with someone unless they want to sleep with them. Gay eye contact. It's a thing.

2. Fingernail Length

Not always accurate, but usually a pretty good indicator.

3. How Does She Feel About Shane from *The L-Word*?

Or gay marriage, or feminism, or any other cultural touchstone for the LGBQ community? Her reaction might be a good indicator as to where she is on the Kinsey scale.

4. Do You Have Chemistry?

Rational human beings don't just invent chemistry, or think they feel it when they don't. There's a difference between having a crush on someone and actually feeling

---

AVOIDING FRIENDCEST

Because the lesbian community can often be small, it's pretty important to have at least a vague idea of whom someone has previously dated or is currently dating, just to avoid awkward overlaps. If you're winging for a friend, do her a favor and either supply or figure out this information. "This is Amanda, who is/was sleeping with Beth." Useful info!

> **One of the nice things about dating someone of your own gender is that you're really free to kind of pick and choose what aspects of a gendered relationship you want and don't want."**

—Mallory, 25, San Francisco

chemistry, right? Chemistry happens when there's that zing, when two people are communicating on the exact same wavelength, when there's a mutual underscoring of sexual tension. If you feel chemistry, then there's a good chance the other person is feeling/sending the same signals too. (Caveat: It is, of course, possible to feel chemistry, mutual chemistry, with someone who otherwise identifies as straight and who perhaps isn't quite comfortable with the idea of dating women. Maybe she'll come around to the idea, but maybe she won't. It's up to you to decide how much to invest in the situation.)

5. Is She Doing the "Hand Tuck"?

You know: one hand casually in the pocket of her jeans. Or one thumb casually looped in her belt hook. Straight girls don't really stand like that.

6. Did You Look Her Up on Facebook?

Ah, yes, Ye Olde Facebook-Stalking method. If you're lucky, you'll find a straight answer (no pun intended?), like "Interested In: Women." Likely, the profile itself will be ambiguous, but taking a gander at her photographs might provide some clues. (Pictures of her with an ex-girlfriend, perhaps?)

7. Ask

The only surefire way to know whether or not someone is interested in women is to ask. There's no foolproof signpost of a person's sexuality. You don't have to make a big deal out of it, and you don't have to come on to her. Just say, "Wait, so do you date women?" the same way you'd ask a straight friend, "Wait, so do you have a boyfriend?"—out of friendly curiosity. If she confirms that she is in fact into women, then you can hit on her, or not.

MORNING-AFTER ETIQUETTE

WOO! YOU hooked up with someone last night. That was great! That was just what the doctor ordered. Except, it's morning now, and he's still sleeping (or pretending to sleep?) about three inches away from you. This is where things get potentially tricky.

How do you handle the morning after a hookup?

First of all, let's just say that if it's strictly a hookup/one-night-stand situation, no one is obligated to spend the night. It's definitely rude to head for the door the second intercourse is over like you just remembered you have an important *Frasier* rerun to watch or something, but after half an hour or so of post-coital cuddling or conversation, it's totally fine to give him a quick kiss on the cheek and skedaddle. Same goes for him.

When you do spend the night together, the next morning becomes a difficult feat of "following the other person's cues." If you both wake up raring to have sex again, then by all means, take advantage. If he, for whatever reason, isn't interested in sex the next day, don't take it too personally. He could have an appointment, a roommate, or a hangover preventing him from a second round. And if *he* wants to have sex again but you don't, just tell him you have to get home/to work, and leave. (A co-worker once told a guy she had to get home in time to listen to *Car Talk*. He got the hint.)

The best way to navigate the morning-after territory, if you want to stay but aren't sure if it's cool, is to make like you're going to leave (i.e., start getting dressed, etc.), and if he then invites you to stay or to go get breakfast, you can stay. But if he smiles at you sleepily from bed, while making no move to invite you back *into it*, and mumbles something like, "K. See ya later," then best to get the hell out of Dodge.

Obvious: If he gets out of bed, YOU HAVE TO GET OUT OF BED TOO!

If you're the one hosting, then it's up to you to send the signals of whether or not you would like your guest to stay. Just remember dating karma. If he asks for a shower, let him take a shower. You might desperately need someone to extend the same courtesy to you someday.

WHEN BEING SINGLE STARTS TO SUCK

So, BEING single is pretty great: You have your friends, your independence, your dalliances with guys. What more could you possibly ask for? Well, a little romance, maybe. Someone with whom to spend cozy weekends at bed-and-breakfasts. Automatic plans for Friday nights, at least for a little while. Someone to split the cost of hotel rooms with, and someone whose shoulder you can fall asleep on on the plane. There's nothing wrong with being single; you know that. But there's nothing wrong with dating a little bit, either. In fact, it could be a nice change of pace, don't you think? Ten signs you're probably ready to get back out there:

1. All of your best dating anecdotes are from a *loong* time ago.

2. You drunkenly hook up with someone almost every weekend, but you can't remember your last sober kiss.

3. The most romantic thing that's happened to you so far this year was when your best friend told you about the amazing blind date she went on.

4. Your Facebook friend from high school, about whom you secretly think, *How did she land a hot boyfriend?*, has broken up with said hot boyfriend and started dating a second hot boyfriend. You're still single and stewing.

5. The mere thought of going on a date gives you anxiety, because you actually have no idea how to act on one.

6. Your friends/co-workers/mom have all said they want to set you up with someone, and they're starting to get insistent. Better take matters into your own hands.

7. Your friends always ask you to babysit/water their plants/have a "casual night in" on Saturday nights because it would never even occur to them that you'd be on a date or have plans. 'Cause let's face it, you never do.

8. Your last date was a bad date. (Replace that awful memory with a better one!)

9. You ended a serious relationship . . . six months ago. Time to get out there.

10. You really, really, really want a relationship. You want it, you gotta do the work! Relationships start with a date.

Chapter 2

HOW TO
GET DATES

WHY
DATING IS IMPORTANT

You don't need a relationship to make you happy. You are the culmination of centuries of women who protested in pantaloons for your right to spend a Tuesday night reading a book with a glass of wine instead of cooking dinner for the family you felt societal pressure to have.

Now's the part where I tell you to go on dates.

Because here's the thing: Dating, in its own quirky little way, is good for you. It's good to have a little romance in your life, a little excitement! Not to mention the fact that dating is a skill that will take you far in life, whether you're looking for a relationship or not.

The skills necessary to become good at dating are insanely useful for other, non-romantic aspects of life. It takes confidence to initiate a conversation with someone you're interested in. It takes gumption to risk rejection by asking him out. It takes an open mind to accept a date from someone, to decide to *really* give him a chance.

It takes tact to end things, and it takes a strong dose of bravery to go in for a kiss. Optimism and persistence don't hurt, either.

If practice makes perfect, then going on dates can turn you into a brave, confident, open, empathetic, tactful person. And let's be honest, going on dates isn't exactly like pulling teeth. If you did a cost/risk analysis, then thirty minutes and a cup of coffee aren't a terribly steep wager: Worst case, you have a funny story for your friends. But usually you'll have a pretty good time, and maybe you'll make out, and maybe you'll date a while, and maybe you'll be inspired to go on another date with someone else.

And maybe you'll fall in love. Sometimes, surrounded as we are by cynicism and sarcasm and previous disappointments and real life, we forget that it's even a possibility. But it is. Maybe you'll force yourself to go on a date and end up falling in love. And what human being doesn't, in the deepest recesses of her soul, want that?

THE ONE-DATE RULE

SO MANY single women are quick to find fault with guys and hesitant to go on a date with someone about whom they feel only lukewarm. The end result is that while there may be plenty of fish in the sea, marine life in the form of potential bachelors dwindles down to an alarmingly low number. An easy solution? Follow the One-Date Rule.

The theory is this: Any guy who gathers up the courage to ask you out (provided he is nice and not, to your knowledge, wanted for any major felonies) deserves the chance to go on one date with you. One date! Let him buy you a cup of coffee in less time than it takes to get a manicure. You might find that this guy you'd sort of discounted is actually kind of hilarious and sweet. And maybe the reasons you wanted

to turn him down in the first place won't be as important to you as you thought.

Or you might drain your iced latte and conclude that, nope, this gentleman is *not* for you. At which point you're done! You gave him a chance, and now you never have to see him again if you don't want to. The important thing here is to expand the list of possible dates, simply by being *open* to the possibility of finding a connection where you didn't think you'd find one.

Remember, there is *no* one, apart from maybe murderers, dictators, and Ponzi schemers, who doesn't deserve at least a chance to buy you coffee and *try* to get you to like him. Besides, it's good dating karma: Someday, you might want some guy to take a chance and say yes to *you*.

 I like meeting new people, so first dates are practice. I take something from it. For me, it's fun."

—Jess, 29, Chicago

"Act confident,
even if you aren't."
—Helen Gurley Brown

You have to kiss
a few frogs before
you meet a prince.

Ain't nothing open
after midnight
'cept legs!

Don't talk about
yourself too much.
Ask him questions.

Gentlemen
offer to pay.

HON

is the

He won't buy
the cow if he can
get the milk for free.

A lady doesn't kiss and tell.

Don't discuss religion,
politics, or money.

Don't eat in front
of your date!

The only time a woman can change
a man is when he's a baby.

"The ability to sit
very still is sexy."
—Sex and the Single Girl

Never call a guy first—
let him call you.

E: *A Matrix*

You have to love yourself in order for someone to love you.

"He's just not that into you if he is not having sex with you."
—*He's Just Not That Into You*

"If he doesn't call, he's not interested. Period."
—*The Rules*

Wait twenty-four hours to follow up after a first date.

Just be yourself!

"Don't drink past two glasses of wine or two cocktails."
—Patti Stanger

Don't be too available.

STY

policy

Always carry an icebreaker with you.

Don't bring up marriage or kids on a first date.

"Don't date a man for too long without a commitment from him."
—*The Rules*

"Don't have sex without monogamy."
—Patti Stanger

Wear red!

It will happen when you least expect it!

The man should love the woman more.

Lie about your "number" if you have to. Subtract a few.

THE SECRET TO A HAPPY DATING LIFE

IF I'VE learned anything over the past two years of writing about dating, it's this: The secret to a happy dating life is to *not worry too much about dating*. A totally frustrating and difficult-to-follow edict, yes, but also the only thing that I can say with complete certainty is true for all women.

If you look at women who are happy with their dating lives, whether they are single or in a relationship, there is one trait they all have in common: a certain *lightness* in their approach to their romantic lives. These women, quite simply, don't seem to sweat it so much. They don't let their relationship status define them. They don't compare their dating lives to those of other women. They don't freak out about being single; they don't worry if a date goes poorly, if a flirtation turns sour.

Perhaps more important, women with happy dating lives aren't overly concerned about how their own actions will be perceived by men: They text when they feel like texting, they have sex when they feel like having sex, they break up when something isn't working. Which is not to say that their lives are devoid of the heartbreak and frustrations normally associated with matters of the heart—of course not. But in general, they take things in stride. Dating is a source of amusement and romance, not of frustration and stress.

Unfortunately, this ineffable quality, this "lightness," is difficult to conjure or to fake. If dating is something that's stressful to you, and if you're frustrated with your current romantic status, it's hard to just *decide* to not worry about it so much. "It will happen when you least expect it" is perhaps the most infuriating thing a single woman who is tired of being single can hear, because, at that point, you're *never* not expecting it. You walk into a party and you hope for it; you scan the room looking for it; you start talking to a guy and, despite all logic or attempts at restraint, you find yourself thinking, *Is this it? Is it him? Is this* finally *it?* When you want something badly, it's hard not to take it seriously.

But what the phrase "it will happen when you least expect it" really means is "it will happen when you just stop worrying about it." It will happen when you let your guard down for a second, when you're thinking about something else, when for a moment all the stress and frustration and *heaviness* part like clouds, and some guy gets a glimpse of the real you that's been hiding underneath. I promise that's the corniest thing you'll read in this book, but it's true, it's true, it's true. It might not be immediate, but once you stop stressing, at some point it will happen.

It's the exact same reason that sometimes "breaking the seal" after a dry spell will usher in a glorious era of promiscuity, and why sometimes you start getting hit on by other guys the second you get a boyfriend. In college, I noticed I had an excellent track record of getting asked out at parties—*but it only happened when I had a crush on someone else.* I'd be so busy scanning the room for the object of my affection and concentrating my (probably intense, probably creepy) thoughts on him that I could be completely light and relaxed and natural with whatever guy I was engaged in conversation with. When, at the end of the night, he'd ask for my number, I was always delightedly caught off-guard. "Was that romantic?? But I wasn't even *thinking* about it! I wasn't even worrying about what was coming out of my mouth, and whether it was attractive or funny or flirty!" But that's what guys are attracted to: someone who's confident and relaxed.

On HowAboutWe dating profiles, we ask people to finish the sentence "I want to be with someone who wants to be ____." For men, the most common answer is overwhelmingly: *happy.* Guys want to be with someone *happy.* It's what they're looking for when they meet you at a party or on a first date, even more than good looks or funny jokes or a smooth, alluring flirtation style. People want to be with someone happy, because if you're with someone happy, then maybe you can be happy, too.

You *have* to figure out a way to be happy without guys, without a date, without sex, without a response to that text or a "like" on a Facebook picture or a flirty exchange on GChat. Because the sooner you lower the stakes on all that, the easier it will be for you to attain. Swear to God. A girl who's depressed, who's given up dating as "hopeless," who thinks all the guys in

We asked daters: If you could go on one date with anyone from history, whom would you choose? (Interestingly, the most popular answers were U.S. presidents. Hail to the Chiefs!)

1. John F. Kennedy
2. Abraham Lincoln
3. Thomas Jefferson
4. Martin Luther King, Jr.
5. Alexander Hamilton
6. Ernest Hemingway
7. John Adams
8. Mark Twain
9. Edgar Allan Poe
10. Elvis

her city "suck" or are "taken already," is simply going to have a much, much harder time finding men. No one wants to be with that girl. You wouldn't want to be with her either.

So how do you practice "lightness" when you're genuinely fed up with dating, when you're seriously afraid you might never meet someone, when you've tried everything and you're sincerely doubtful that a hippy-dippy state of being is going to dramatically change your dating life?

It's a slow process, but you have to try to get to the point where you are okay just being yourself. It might be hard work! It might take a long time! It might mean investing in your friends, in your hobbies, in whatever it is you do that makes you happy and relaxed. But eventually, the change will be apparent. People *will* notice something different about you.

Just don't worry about it so much.

Take it lightly.

FIVE SIMPLE WAYS TO CHILL THE FUCK OUT ABOUT DATING

1. **When you're out socializing, try to have a conversation with a guy you aren't necessarily attracted to or interested in.**
Don't zoom in only on potential dates.

2. **Be open to casual dating and new experiences.**
Not every guy has to be a potential boyfriend, and not every boyfriend needs to be a potential husband.

3. **Look for new friends—don't just cast around for a boyfriend.**
People can enrich your life in non-romantic ways, too!

4. **Join an intramural league, a book club, a language class.**
NOT because you might meet guys there, but because these things are enriching to *you* and *your* life . . . and because it's good to have non–dating-related evening plans every now and then. And because people who have hobbies and interests are more interesting than people who don't.

5. **Go on more first dates! Say yes to people you wouldn't otherwise say yes to.**
It seems counterintuitive, sure, but the more dates you go on, the less you tend to freak out and get nervous about them . . . .

FLIRTING

DATING IS good for you on a number of different levels, but flirting is just *fun*. It can entertain you while you're stuck in an airport, it can liven up a mundane workday, it can get you a round of free drinks, it can cheer you up when you're having a shitty day, and, most important for our purposes, it can quickly build a rapport between two strangers, leading to that elusive phenomenon, a *spark*. You'll probably, for whatever reason, have to stop dating eventually, but flirting? You can flirt till you're a hundred and one.

And flirting is easy! It's mostly just eye contact followed by banter and strategic touching. Low-key, low-risk, and pretty essential to an active dating life.

There's an endless variety of ways to flirt, based on the situation, the person you're trying to flirt with, your own personality, etc. But if we're talking basics here, the most important weapons in your flirting arsenal are your eyes. Yep, it may seem ridiculously simple, but the easiest and fastest way to convey interest in someone is by simply *looking* at him. As city dwellers, we've been conditioned to avoid eye contact whenever humanly possible—on the subway, on the elevator, on the street. So the mere act of catching someone's eye and *not* immediately looking away unequivocally proves that you've taken notice of him and want him to take notice of you right back.

So that's the building block; that's how you get someone's attention. From there, you can do any iteration of eye contact/smile/ light touch to get someone's attention and start a conversation. Perhaps over the years you've perfected an elaborate, almost Machiavellian way of initiating contact with a guy. Anything can work, if pulled off with enough confidence. But if you ever find yourself at a loss, go back to the basics: Look at him, maintain his gaze, and smile.

Once you've established contact with a guy, flirting usually takes the form of witty repartee (or not-so-witty repartee . . . you'd be amazed at how inane a conversation can get when two people are goofy-in-like with each other), gentle teasing, light touching, making cheesy jokes/laughing extra-hard at the cheesy jokes, etc.

Remember, when you're flirting, you're indirectly expressing sexual interest in a friendly/playful way. If you're worried about coming off as *friendly* and not *flirty*, use body language/contact to express what your conversation isn't (and vice versa). Make sure that you're giving him your full attention, that you're turned toward him, that you're relaxed, that you're standing close, etc.

The most important thing flirting does is build attraction and tension between two people. You want everything you're doing to suggest intimacy, but you have to start small and work your way up. It's why going up to a guy and just kissing him isn't *quite* as hot as starting slow and kissing at the end of the night. (I'm sure there are guys who will disagree here, but I'll stand by it.) Start small, and give yourself somewhere to go.

A VERY BASIC FLIRTING TECHNIQUE THAT EVERYONE CAN MASTER

1. **Establish your target (usually a stranger), and make quick eye contact three times.**
(You don't need to maintain eye contact as long as he sees you look at him.)

2. **Find a reason to move past the target to the other side of the room.**
(Bathroom break? Smoke break? Another drink? Another conversation?) Make your way in his direction, and as soon as you're close enough, *hold eye contact.*

3. **Keep holding eye contact! And right when you're moving past him, smile.**
Maintain eye contact until you're almost past him. And then continue on your way.

That's it. That's all you have to do. If he's available, he'll approach you. And no one can accuse you of *throwing* yourself at him—after all, all you did was walk past him on your way to somewhere else. Foolproof.

IF YOU'RE TOO SHY...

I F SHYNESS AND insecurity are things you struggle with, try striking up conversations in less-pressure-filled situations. The point is to just practice talking to strangers—the more you do it, the more confident you'll feel. Head to a local bar on a weekday, when there won't be too many people (and when it's perfectly acceptable to grab a drink by yourself after a long day), and talk to the bartender. Force yourself to go to that random party an acquaintance invited you to on Facebook, even though you won't know any of the other attendees. Challenge yourself to stay for at least twenty-five minutes—*without looking at your cell phone*. If you're still freaked out by the thought of initiating a conversation, try flirting online. Comment on someone's Facebook picture or status, forward an article, or instant-message him. Of course, you'll need to transfer this flirtation to real life soon enough, but flirting online can be a great way to break the ice.

IF YOU'RE TOO FORWARD...

I T'S FRUSTRATING TO hear that your approach to guys is "too forward" or "too aggressive." But the thing is, you can intimidate a guy by coming on too strong, in the same way guys can intimidate women by being too aggressive in their approach. A little subtlety, a little coyness, is an important part of early flirtation, regardless of gender. Give him a chance to play too. Think of flirting like passing a hot potato. Make a move, or give him a signal that lets him know—unequivocally—that you're interested in him. Now, what's he going to do about it? Let *him* take the next step. The guy who doesn't make the next move? You wouldn't want him anyway. You need someone who can play at your speed.

SMILE!

Make eye contact

Show confidence

- A mild spill always gets attention. But you cannot be drunk AT ALL for this to be charming.
- Talk college football.
- You gotta bust balls a little bit.

Laugh

- Bring him cookies.
- Talk about work (but not too much!)
- Talk about sex in a totally open, frank, funny, non-personal way.

Talk to him

- Compliment his shoes!
- Ask advice on what beer to order.
- Make fun of yourself.
- Order a specific, semi-obscure Scotch, like Laphroig or Talisker.

Look, then look away

- Share your passion.
- Mention cars.
- Tuck his tag back into his shirt.
- Wear liquid eyeliner!!!

Signature **FLIRTING MOVES**

What "signature moves" are other women using to flirt with guys? HowAboutWe.com polled women about their flirting styles, and the answers proved that when it comes to getting someone's attention, there's more than one way to skin a cat, so to speak. Here are some of the most popular answers. (The size of each circle is in proportion to the popularity of the response.)

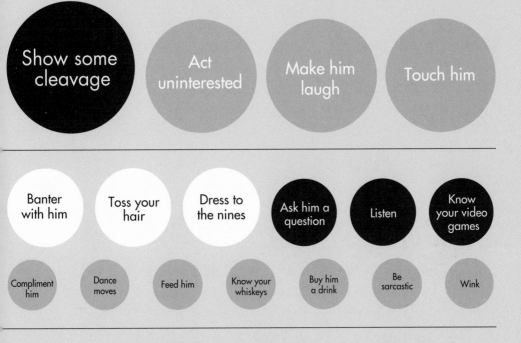

Show some cleavage

Act uninterested

Make him laugh

Touch him

Banter with him

Toss your hair

Dress to the nines

Ask him a question

Listen

Know your video games

Compliment him

Dance moves

Feed him

Know your whiskeys

Buy him a drink

Be sarcastic

Wink

- Go up to him and guess his name.
- Tell a joke.
- Bite your lip.
- Make him jealous.
- Toss HIS hair.

- Casually tell him he smells nice.
- Give him an over-the-shoulder smile.
- Flirt with his friends.
- Pinch his butt.

- Karaoke. Period.
- Wear red.
- Wear pink Chuck Taylors.
- Wear a little black dress.
- Challenge him to a game of pool or darts or cards.

- Play footsie.
- Talk about how much you're not interested in dating.
- Ask for his help.
- Be happy.
- Act like one of the guys.

THE ART OF PLAYING IT COOL

L ET ME JUST say that I categorically don't believe in playing it cool. What is wrong with letting someone you know you like him? As if liking someone is some big, repulsive secret you have to keep to yourself at all costs. Please! Playing it cool is basically why we are the mumblecore generation, why our romantic exchanges consist of "hey what are you up 2" on GChat.

That said, I do understand that it's hard to be the only one *not* playing it cool in a world where people's romantic impulses tend to be a little . . . tempered.

The tricky part of trying to play it cool when you're secretly hot for someone is that it's way too easy to go to the opposite extreme. You're so aware of your attraction for someone that you feel everyone else must be, too, so you tone it way, way, down. Suddenly you're avoiding eye contact, you're giving curt replies, and you're probably coming off as a bit . . . mean. And definitely not interested.

Worried that you're being too flirty or not flirty enough? Check out the handy guide on the opposite page.

> **I don't like the game of who can seem less interested but still interested at the same time. You both get to the place where you're not sure you really like each other because you've both been so aloof."**
>
> —Rose, 23, Chicago

BITCHY AND/OR UNINTERESTED		FRIENDLY		FLIRTY		DESPERATE
	VS.		VS.		VS.	
Not saying hello when he arrives at a party.		Greeting him, or responding when he greets you.		Going over to him and saying, "I was wondering when you'd get here!"		Rushing to him the second he arrives and not leaving his side all night.
Refusing to follow him back or grant his friend request on Facebook.		Following back or accepting his friend request if he friends you first.		Sending him a cute message or tweet.		Following him on all possible social-media platforms the very night you meet him.
Going up to him at a bar and negging him.		Going up to him at a bar and introducing yourself.		Going up to him at a bar and challenging him to a game of darts or pool.		Going up to him at a bar and suggesting he buy you a drink.
Carefully keeping your hands to yourself and avoiding any physical contact.		Giving him a hug at the end of a conversation, or a slap on the back for emphasis.		Touching his arm, leg, or back throughout the conversation; touching hands when you hand each other something; playing footsie.		Hanging onto his arm, sitting on his lap, seeking constant physical contact that isn't reciprocated.
Ignoring an email or text.		Responding to an email or text the next day.		Responding to an email or text that day.		Responding to an email or text the second he sends it.

DO LOOKS MATTER?

O F COURSE THEY DO, and anyone who tells you otherwise is either naive, delusional, or criminally attractive herself. (Have you noticed that? It's always your prettiest friend who sweetly informs you that it's what's on the *inside* that matters.)

The inside *does* matter, but not in the first thirty seconds of knowing someone, and hot girls have a much easier time of immediately getting noticed. Whatever. No one said biology is fair.

But before you resign yourself to a lifetime of spinsterhood and/or plastic surgery, here's the good news: There is lots of evidence that looking like a perfect ten isn't *as* important as we all maybe assume.

In 2011, OkCupid's blog did a quick study of the effect of physical beauty on an online dating site. The study showed that, yes, the total knockouts did get a significantly higher frequency of messages. I'm sure you're shocked.

But! Apart from the perfect tens, the surprising runners-up in terms of message quantity were girls who wouldn't necessarily be considered conventionally attractive.

Now obviously, in most cases, beauty is a highly subjective thing that's hard to quantify. But the OkCupid study found that girls who rated somewhat lower in terms of general-consensus attractiveness tended to have a specific part of the population who found them REALLY attractive, and were more likely to receive messages. Girls with unusual (or divisive) traits, such as tattoos, piercings, or a few extra curves often did *just* as well as the supermodel types. **In other words, don't worry too much about trying to fit a (nonexistent) male ideal: You're somebody's cup of tea, just as you are.** Swear to God.

Feeling pretty good about yourself? Here's more nice news: A 1997 research study by Mehrabian and Blum discovered that the qualities that men and women find *most* attractive in each other are all changeable qualities. (For reference: A "changeable" quality can be hairstyle, fitness, clothing, etc. Some stable qualities include face shape, eye color, and height.)

The study found that the qualities that were rated "most attractive" all fell under the category of self-care: for example, grooming, clothing, healthy weight, etc. Which basically means how you present yourself is more important than how you actually *look*. And luckily, there are some pretty simple and effective ways to look like the best, hottest version of yourself.

How to

BE MORE ATTRACTIVE

IN FIVE EASY STEPS

1

GROOMING

Let's assume you've got the basics covered: brushed hair, deodorant, fresh breath. Some other things that are easy to let slip or not notice: dirty hair, runny/smeared makeup, chipped/messy nails.

2

CLOTHING

It really doesn't matter *what* you wear, as long as it's clean, relatively wrinkle-free, and, above all, *fits you*. (Don't wear anything that needs incessant, and obvious, *adjusting*.)

3

POSTURE

The easiest, cheapest, and best thing you can do for your appearance is to simply *stand up a little straighter*. (Do I sound like your mother right now? I sound like *my* mother right now.) But you'll look confident, taller, slimmer!

4

FITNESS

You don't have to run out and get a personal trainer for a total body overhaul. You just have to, again, take relatively good care of yourself. Get the blood pumping.

5

FACIAL EXPRESSION

The 1997 Mehrabian and Blum study found that "pleasantness" rated surprisingly high on the list of attractive physical traits. So try to smile, or at least keep your face as pleasantly neutral as befits the situation. (Don't grin like a maniac during a funeral, for instance. Also, don't pick up guys at a funeral.)

WHAT GUYS NOTICE

about women

1. CUTE FACE

Contrary to what pop culture would have you believe, most guys say they notice a woman's face before they really look at her body.

2. BODY TYPE

Once a friendly face is ascertained, guys do tend to notice whether "a woman is demonstrably out of shape," as Jack, 27, from Jersey City, delicately put it. "I would notice breasts and/or ass before I notice triceps . . . although nice triceps are actually good."

3. CLOTHING

Guys don't critique clothing so much as they try to analyze it. How a woman is dressed says a lot about her personal style, branding, and wealth level. "I want someone who knows how to dress well for her style," said Chris, 24, from Brooklyn. "Not necessarily expensively, but that she has some kind of good aesthetic and it fits how she acts."

4. DEMEANOR

Bradney, 26, from L.A., has one thing he notices above all others when it comes to women: "Is she loud?" Another guy confessed he notices if a woman is "overly aggressive in speech or mannerism for the setting."

5. ENTOURAGE

Guys always take note of whether a girl is surrounded by men or women. "If a girl has a ton of guy friends, it helps you know that if she's being nice to you, it may not mean she's into you," said one guy.

6. EYE CONTACT

Almost every guy brought up eye contact. "I don't know, girls have a way of making eyes look sexy briefly but then back to normal again," said Patrick, 26, from Boston. "Ability and desire to hold eye contact is a big signal."

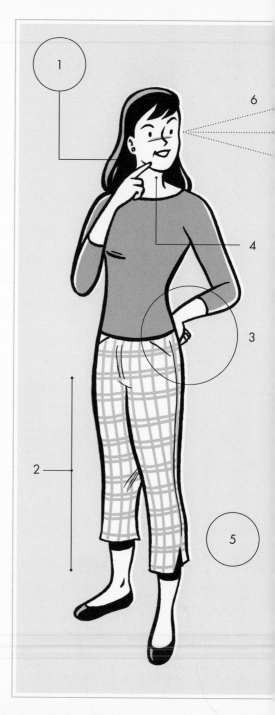

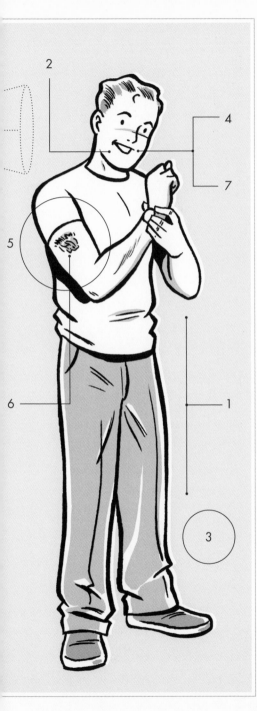

WHAT WOMEN NOTICE
about guys

1. IF HE'S HOT
It's not the most important quality a guy can have, but it's probably the first we notice.

2. IF HE HAS FACIAL HAIR
Some girls dig it, some girls don't. As Erica, 30, from New York City put it: "If I notice facial hair, it probably means I don't like it."

3. IF HE'S ALONE
Is he with a girl? Then interest is lessened: He's probably taken. Is he with a group of friends? Fun, good to know he's social. Is he alone? Then maybe worth an approach.

4. IF HE HAS AN ACCENT
Bonus points. No matter where from.

5. IF HE'S TONED
Not a prerequisite, or even something we notice from across the room. But if, upon closer inspection, we see some defined arms, well, sweet.

6. ACCESSORIES
Gold chain? Livestrong bracelet? Hemp bracelet? Tattoo? All telling signs. "Chains around the neck scream Danny Zuko from *Grease*, which may not be a bad thing for some people, but is a big turnoff for me," said Madeline, 26, from New York City.

7. IF HE LAUGHS EASILY
A guy who laughs easily seems at ease with himself and charming. It's appealing! Brooding is rarely as sexy in real life as it is on TV.

YOUR DATING POOL

YOU KNOW how to flirt. You know how to get a guy's attention. You're so charming that anyone with a brain would want to spend copious amounts of time with you. Now it's just a matter of actually meeting people. Which, depending on where you live, your level of social activity, and how outgoing you are, might be easier said than done. As much as we may all dream of meeting someone by reaching for the same obscure record at a record store, or accidentally getting into the same cab, meet-cutes like that mostly just happen in romantic comedies.

Yes, one bummer about adulthood is that it can become difficult to meet people once you've settled into your work/friends routine.

And if there were any eligible guys in your office or friend circle, you would have dated them by now. (And maybe you already have—we'll get to recycling later.)

If you want to actively date, you're going to have to actively try to meet new people. This might mean joining an intramural sports group, dragging yourself out on a night when you'd really rather stay home, or asking friends to introduce you to any promising single acquaintants they might know. The more you put yourself in new situations, the more new people you're going to meet. I talked to a girl recently who complained about never meeting guys. When I asked her what she does in her free time, she told me she works out at

> **I would honestly suggest that a woman try to make some guy friends. Just being around guys and talking to them can help to make you more laid-back around guys and to realize that they're not on a pedestal."**

—Christine, 26, Boston

an all-female gym and sings in a choir: not exactly hot spots for young single men.

I'm not saying you should immediately run out and join any testosterone-fueled activity in the mere hope of meeting dudes. But if your knitting circle isn't widening your dating pool, make sure you're putting yourself in *some* situations where you're interacting with members of the opposite sex. A volunteer group, a language class, a dodgeball league, trivia night at a local bar, or even just happy hour in a different part of town can all be easy and fun ways to expand your social circle. And what if you don't meet anyone? You'll still have fun, and be a more interesting person, the more new things you try.

But you don't really need to overhaul your extracurricular life in order to meet someone (though it indubitably helps). Sometimes it's just a matter of taking the initiative in everyday situations.

It's a little bit corny, but think of it this way: Every time you leave your house, there's a chance you might meet the next great love of your life. But you might have to help things along by getting up the courage to talk to him.

How to

MEET SOMEONE...

AT THE COFFEE SHOP	AT THE GYM

"Would you watch my stuff for a minute?"

Sure he will! And then you can start a conversation when you get back from the bathroom/getting some napkins that you didn't really need.

Get a really huge brownie.

And then say you can't finish the whole thing, and offer to share. (Even if—who are we kidding—of course you could finish the whole thing; you have a stomach of steel.)

Comment on the book he's reading.

Which you know ALL about (because you secretly Wikipedia'd it before making your move).

"Do you need a refill?"

Simple and elegant. On your way to the counter for your second cup of coffee, just stop by the person's table and casually, as if it's nothing, ask him if he needs a refill.

Race him.

Turn to the guy on the bike next to you in Spinning class and say, "Race you." Worst-case scenario: You get a better workout. Best-case scenario: You get a date.

Ask for a spot.

Most people won't mind helping someone out for a few minutes in the weight room, and it's a perfectly normal request. You can make small talk during sets, and if he doesn't seem interested by the end of the reps, you leave it at that.

Watch what he's watching.

If you're both on the cardio machines watching the same TV show, it's easy enough to make a comment about what you're watching—or at least make eye contact over shared reactions (laughter/surprise, etc.).

Use the mirror.

The mirror walls in gyms are ostensibly for checking out your form—but obviously they're great for checking out *other* people as well. Don't be afraid to smile at someone cute if you make accidental eye contact. If he holds your gaze or smiles back, find him later and say hello. (If he looks away, leave him alone! Some people go to the gym just to zone out. Respect that!)

ON PUBLIC TRANSPORTATION

Don't wear your city armor.

You know. The headphones, the book, the cell phone, and the scowl that you usually have with you on public transportation in order to discourage any weirdos from trying to make conversation or even eye contact with you. Leave them in your bag for once. You'll look more approachable, and be more aware of who might be worth approaching.

Ask for directions.

Easy. "Is this train running express?" "How can I get to X?" Lots of guys are hesitant about talking to a girl on public transport for fear of seeming creepy (rightly so, actually), but if *you* initiate, it gives him the okay to talk to you.

Make an observation.

Comment on his shoes, his book, the delay, the traffic, the weather. It really doesn't matter what you say—initiating a conversation on public transit is *so* rare that the mere act of doing it conveys interest. At the end of the conversation, tell him it was the best commute you've had in a while and that you hope to see him again sometime. If he's not a dolt, he'll ask for your number to make sure you do. (You can also just give it to him.)

Be bold.

You really won't see this person again (unless you really *are* in a romantic comedy!), so you might as well be bold for once in your life. Walk up to him and say something to the effect of "I'm going to spare myself the hassle of making a Missed Connection ad for you. Here's my number."

AT THE BOOKSTORE

Park in the "New Releases" section.

People are much more likely to go to the new releases than "Military History" or any other niche spot you could linger in. It's also really easy to ask, "Have you read this yet?" or, conversely, say, "Oh, I just read that—it was amazing, you should definitely get it!"

Pick up an employee.

You're getting a gift for your mom. She likes . . . fiction? Maybe? Keep it vague, so the employee will spend a lot of time helping you find the perfect book.

Go to a reading.

Book readings are amazing—because they are free, because they're something people very commonly and not-weirdly attend on their own, and because there's a perfect built-in conversation topic. Often there is wine, and you can also easily strike up a conversation with the people in line who are waiting to get a book signed.

Try the bookstore café.

If you get into great conversation with someone over a mutual favorite author, it's easy to invite him to get a cup of coffee if it's two aisles over. The more casual, the better. Even if you haven't met anyone yet, the perk of bookstore cafés is that there are *never* enough tables—perfect excuse to share a table with someone cute.

ON RECYCLING

EVEN IF you're meeting new guys left and right, the temptation to recycle a hookup is pretty hard to pass up, should the correct occasion present itself.

The joy of recycling is this: You guys already know each other, already have a rapport you can easily slip back into, already know what the other is like in bed. When you're recycling someone, you can skip all the preliminaries and get straight to the good stuff. It's familiar, it's comforting, and, frankly, it's just less *effort* than starting from scratch with someone entirely new.

There's no real harm in recycling, as long as you do it selectively. You can only recycle the same guy so many times; his recycling value diminishes with each use, as each successive reunion gets imbued with more and more layers of drama. And if you're *only* recycling guys, well, you're gonna run out of men eventually. Get some new guys into the mix—you can recycle them later, too.

OKAY TO RECYCLE:	BETTER NOT TO RECYCLE:
One-off hookups, short-term ex-boyfriends, crushes from your hometown, that guy you have chemistry with but the timing never quite works out, a friend with whom you formerly had benefits, that cute bartender you were hooking up with for a while.	Serious ex-boyfriends. The guy you were in love with but who was only interested in hooking up. The guy your friends were sick to death of hearing about six months ago.

TURNING A HOOKUP INTO SOMETHING MORE

TURNING A hookup into something more isn't impossible, but you do have to be fine with the possibility that he might not *want* something more right now.

If it's a one-night stand, say something before you or he leaves: "Hey, if you want to hang out sometime, we should grab a bite to eat/go see a movie/get a drink." It's important to specify an activity, so that your invitation seems more date-y than sex-y. (Don't say, "This was fun; we should do it again sometime" unless you're strictly referring to the sex part.) Another, perhaps simpler way to parlay a hookup into a date scenario is to simply suggest breakfast. After sharing a meal and conversation, it's easy to suggest hanging out again soon.

If you want to pursue something more serious with a guy you've been hooking up with on a recurring basis, you're gonna need to have a conversation with him, and this conversation **cannot take place in bed.** If you ask someone if he wants to date you right after you have sex with him—or worse, during—you might get a less-than-honest answer (because he doesn't want to hurt your feelings while you're both naked and vulnerable, or because the glow of orgasm makes him say things he doesn't mean). Or he could give you a completely honest but ultimately disappointing answer, which will then make you feel *horrible,* given that you are still in bed with the man. (Just *try* to casually brush off a rejection when you're under the sheets and naked.)

At some point—when you're *not* in bed together—ask him if he's ever thought that this could be something more. Be honest with him, and say that you like hooking up with him *and* his company, and think maybe you should try seeing where this goes. If he agrees with you, then plan to go on a real *date*—we're talking at least two hours of quality time together *before* sex. If he says no, try not to take it too personally, but stop hooking up with him. I know! He's a great hookup. I know! You really like him. But if you want something more and you know that he doesn't, you're not on level playing fields anymore, and he ceases to be an eligible hookup buddy. Casual sex only works if the stakes are exactly the same for both players.

THE GRAY AREA

I T'S ARGUABLY one of the most exciting but also most confusing parts of dating: that in-between time after you've met someone and before you've actually gone on a date with him. The gray area. You're *pretty* sure he likes you. But you've been wrong before. And even if he does like you (which, let's face it, he probably does), how do you parlay heavy flirting into an actual date?

At some point, someone has to ask the other person out. Traditionally, this is done by the guy. But asking someone out is really super-terrifying, so he's probably only going to do it if he's absolutely, positively, beyond a doubt sure that there's a pretty good chance you'll say yes. Otherwise he may chicken out. This is why it's essential that you make it pretty clear to the guy you're flirting with that you're receptive to the idea of his asking for your number or inviting you to hang out.

And even then he *still* might not be able to pull the trigger (or he might be completely clueless as to your interest in him). In that case, take matters into your own hands and ask him out yourself. You don't have to do it immediately. But if after two weeks of flirt-texting you're frustrated that it's leading nowhere, take the bull by the horns and invite him to hang out with you.

There's a sneaky way to ask a guy out by actually throwing the ball back in his court, and it's this: Simply *invite* him to invite you to go out. Say: "Let me know if you want to grab a bite sometime." That way you're suggesting the date, but he's the one who will have to actually ask you out . . . by "letting you know" that, yes, he does want to grab a bite.

Another super-simple way to ask a guy out is to always keep an eye out for great date activities—even before you have the date. If there's a concert or a play that you want to check out, buy two tickets. That way, if you happen to meet someone, you can just say, truthfully, "I have an extra ticket to ___ next week. Do you wanna come?" And keeping on top of events and activities in your area is great conversation fodder that can easily be transitioned into an invitation. ("Are you doing anything for Halloween? I've been reading about these ghost tours on the East Side that seem insane ....")

EASY WAYS TO "SEAL THE DEAL" AT THE END OF A CONVERSATION

1. "Here, let me give you my card."

2. "You're on Facebook, yeah? I'm gonna friend you."

3. "I work in/live in ____. Let me know if you're ever in the neighborhood; we can grab a drink."

4. "Will I see you around here again?"

5. "Give me your email address— I wanna send you the name of that band when I remember it."

6. "What are you up to the rest of the night?"

Should You
ASK HIM OUT?

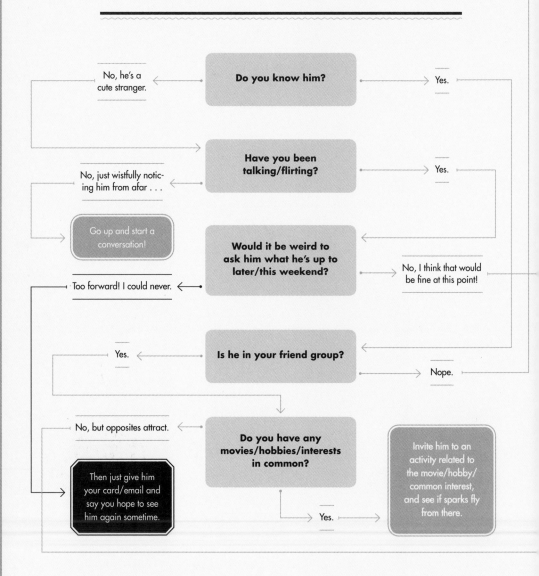

No, he's a cute stranger.

Do you know him?

Yes.

Have you been talking/flirting?

Yes.

No, just wistfully noticing him from afar . . .

Go up and start a conversation!

Would it be weird to ask him what he's up to later/this weekend?

No, I think that would be fine at this point!

Too forward! I could never.

Yes.

Is he in your friend group?

Nope.

No, but opposites attract.

Then just give him your card/email and say you hope to see him again sometime.

Do you have any movies/hobbies/interests in common?

Invite him to an activity related to the movie/hobby/ common interest, and see if sparks fly from there.

Yes.

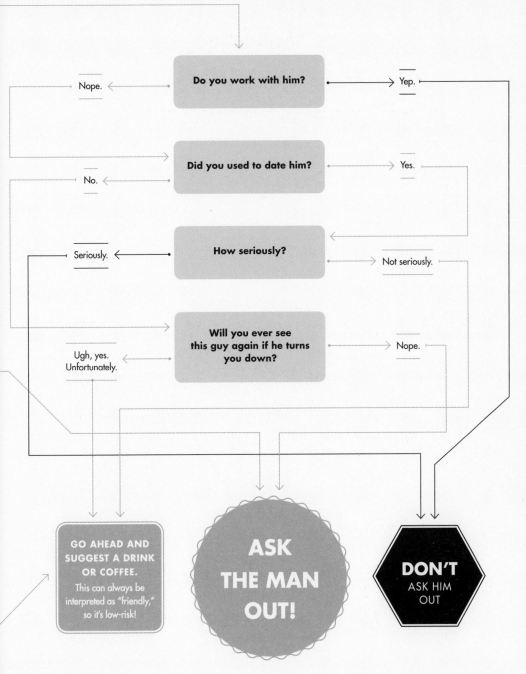

Do you work with him?

Nope. ← → Yep.

Did you used to date him?

No. ← → Yes.

How seriously?

Seriously. ← → Not seriously.

Will you ever see this guy again if he turns you down?

Ugh, yes. Unfortunately. ← → Nope.

GO AHEAD AND SUGGEST A DRINK OR COFFEE.
This can always be interpreted as "friendly," so it's low-risk!

ASK THE MAN OUT!

DON'T ASK HIM OUT

From the Trenches

WHEN HE ASKS FOR YOUR NUMBER BUT DOESN'T CALL

Girls complain about this happening to them all the time. I don't have an explanation, because it's happened to me, too. So I went directly to the source and asked *guys* why the hell this always happens. Their answers were enlightening . . . sort of.

"I feel like more of a dick if I *don't* ask for her number than if I ask and don't call. Much easier to just never call from a distance than to not ask for her number when you're standing across from her and you think she wants you to."

—KEVIN, 26, NEW YORK CITY

"It's a drunk masculine obligation to get at least ONE number."

—DANIEL, 26, SAN DIEGO

"We'd have to think of something to say once we call. This is very difficult."

—PATRICK, 28, NEW YORK CITY

"Isn't it nicer to sit in the joy of having gotten a number than to contact that number and risk feeling rejected or ignored?"

—DUNCAN, 35, AUSTIN

"Many girls give out their number because they really just want the guy to go away but want to be nice. We know this."

—MASON, 28, BOSTON

"Getting a girl to give you her number is a confidence-booster, and sometimes that's all a guy is looking for."

—MATT, 33, MILWAUKEE

"I have a feeling most guys ask for a number because they're 'supposed to' and then realize they can't even remember the last time they called to order a pizza, let alone ask a girl on a date. It's DATED."

—JAMES, 25, NEW YORK CITY

"The basic answer is simple: We feel obligated to."

—DAVID, 30, BALTIMORE

Okay, so what have we learned here? Men are sometimes disingenuous wusses? But more important: Just because a guy gets your number doesn't mean he's going to call. If you really want to talk to this guy again, make sure *you* get *his* number—or email—too.

TEXTING SURVIVAL SKILLS

KATIE HEANEY, *Text-Etiquette Expert, Buzzfeed*

WHEN I have a crush on someone, these are the things I do with my phone:

1. Try to resist texting him, 2. try to resist even *thinking* about texting him, 3. text him something useless anyway, and 4. wait for him to respond while clutching my phone, as though if I squeezed it hard enough, it would produce a reply. The only way to get through it, I have found, is to make my best friend take my phone away from me. Of course, that doesn't really work either, because every fifteen minutes or so, I will ask her to go into her room, where she's hidden it, and check to see if I have any new messages. It is exhausting for everyone involved. To help control this little issue, I've pulled together the following guidelines to look to whenever the urge to text strikes. I suggest you keep these somewhere important, like inside your first-aid kit.

If you like someone, text him or her with purpose. Your premise can be thin, but you have to at least make an attempt. There will be no "how are you/how was your day/how was work" texting in the early stages of a possible relationship. This is not flirtation; it is too vague, too existentialist. Having a topic or a point helps you have something to flirt around.

Know this: "I don't text" is no longer an acceptable declaration for someone to make. (Not everyone must love it, but surely everyone, if he or she is dating, must DO it.) Be wary of the shadow figures who say these ridiculous things.

Be patient, at first. If you text your crush and he takes a while to respond, it really could be because he is busy or at work. However, if someone consistently goes hours/days before responding to you (or responds only sometimes), this person is likely either too disrespectful or not interested enough for you to risk carpal tunnel over. Unfortunately, people cannot be texted into submission.

Should a crush ever send you a message consisting of any of the following expressions, emoticons, or solitary letters:

"wats up"

"k"

"Nah" or "eh"

":p"

…then you must promise me that you will abandon that particular mission at once. Your time on this planet is just too precious.

Remember that texting alone never made or broke a relationship. There has to be other good stuff going for something to happen. It's like building a fire: Flint (texting) can help you start it, but you aren't going to get anywhere without a bunch of wood. (This should help ease the texting pressure, but I know that it probably won't.)

Chapter 3

TAKING THE
ONLINE PLUNGE

ONLINE DATING

Is a Great Supplement for

EVERY HAPPY DATING LIFE

"I don't have anything against online dating;
it's just not for me."

THUS QUOTH, LIKE, every other single girl I talk to about dating. And I get it! There's something intimidating about signing up for an online-dating site. It's a little like Officially Registering as a Single Person.

It's fine for your roommate, it's fine for your divorced aunt, but *you* aren't ready to "resort" to it yet. You want to meet your soul mate in a romantic and organic fashion; you don't want to pick him out of a lineup of profiles that you flip through with all the enthusiasm of someone flipping through a SkyMall catalog. (*"No. No. Never. Maybe. No. Yes. No."*)

Here's the thing, though: Necessity is the mother of invention, and when it comes

to modern dating, especially in cities, there is a huge need for an effective way to meet potential partners. It's *hard* to meet new people as adults, and once you weed out the takens, the gays, and the assholes, your dating pool is significantly smaller. Never again will you have the sheer volume of single men to meet as when you were a freshman in college. (And what were you doing during those four years? Studying? Establishing lifelong female friendships? Youth is wasted on the young!)

So let's talk about the kinds of guys you'll find on an online-dating site. Any dating site worth its salt definitely has a healthy dose of, well, let's just say it, weirdos that you'd never

> **"What I like about online dating is that you can be specific about what you are looking for. I want a tall male between the ages of 27 and 37 who likes dogs and cats and happens to be Jewish and—BAM!—there they are!"**
>
> —Megan, 27, San Diego

want to date. But there are also normal, nice guys who, spurred on by their friends or tequila or pictures of their ex looking happy, create a profile for themselves. Guys who, like you, may simply be too busy with work, friends, and life right now to be constantly going out and meeting people.

And here's something else to think about: You never know whom you're not meeting. Sure, you've got your guys at work, your friends of friends, the men who hang out at your preferred bar, gym, Chinese takeout. But there could be someone *beyond perfect for you* living just across town, someone you'd never have met had you not decided to take a more proactive approach to your dating life.

Honestly, why risk *not* meeting someone great? Any smart dater will diversify her options as best she can. So continue to go to parties, continue to flirt at bars, continue to make small talk at cafés, and agree to get fixed up by your friends. But set up a profile, too. Because online dating is not only an effective way of meeting people, it's also a good way to clarify what you're looking for, and answering the questions on the profile is a helpful exercise in self-expression. (How you present yourself online may lead you to reflect on how you present yourself in person.)

Online dating is *not* a last resort; it's a risk-free supplement to an active and happy dating life.

FIVE REASONS IT'S TIME TO BITE THE BULLET AND TRY ONLINE DATING

(EVEN THOUGH YOU SWORE YOU NEVER WOULD)

---

1. **You're too busy to meet new people.**
Life is crazy right now, and you just don't have *time* to go out and expand your social circle. Online dating makes it easy to fit dating into your schedule, 'cause you can message throughout the day and browse profiles from the comfort of your own couch.

2. **You're totally over the bar-hookup scene.**
Bars have historically been your go-to for meeting guys, but now you've gotten to the point where some romance before midnight would be nice for a change.

3. **If you get set up one more time, you might have to kill somebody.**
Do your friends really know whom you should date? Rarely. Ultimately, it's better to do the legwork and screening yourself.

4. **If you get your friends involved, it can be kind of fun.**
To anyone who's never had a giggly, alcohol-fueled session of filling out a profile and checking out potential dates with friends: You are missing out.

5. **You just need to get your dating confidence back.**
Sometimes all you need is a really good date, or even just a really good message from someone cute, to remind you how fun dating can be, and how attractive, desirable, and awesome you are.

The Odds Online

ARE IN YOUR FAVOR

| RATIO OF GIRLS TO GUYS IN MAJOR METROPOLITAN AREAS | RATIO OF GIRLS TO GUYS DATING ONLINE |

 1. **New York City**
111 : 100

 2. **Boston**
105 : 100

 3. **Chicago**
106 : 100

 4. **Los Angeles**
101 : 100

 5. **Washington, D.C.**
113 : 100

91 : 100*

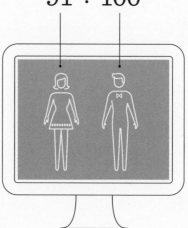

* average of 15 top online-dating-site ratios

ONLINE-DATING
SUCCESS STORIES

"I tried online dating because I wanted to meet someone with the same interests as me (*Lord of the Rings*—check, loves TED lectures—check, interested in business—check) and a similar personality. In a post-college world, where it is so difficult to meet people on the street, it was nice to see a summary of someone and say yea or nay. I met an amazing guy on one of my first online dates, and he's moving in next week!!"

—MISA, 26, SAN FRANCISCO

"'I will NEVER online-date. It takes the happenstance out of love.' That is exactly what I said to my friend after one of his many attempts to get me to jump into the Internet dating pool. Late one night, I broke down a little and set up a profile on HowAboutWe. After a few months of my friend's sending me profile after profile (I refused to even look at most of them), I finally gave in and hit 'intrigued' on the date idea of a seemingly nice guy on the Lower East Side. I made a deal with my friend that if I went out on one stupid, pointless online date, he would

never be able to hound me again! I agreed to meet my first-ever online date for a glass of wine, thinking I could find some excuse to duck out early. The moment I turned around to greet him, I felt like kicking myself for waiting so long to find what I had been looking for. We've been together ever since our first date."

—DELANEY, 25, AUSTIN

"I was initially freaked out by the idea of dating online, probably just because it wasn't something many of my friends had done. But I wasn't meeting people out at bars anymore, and I was tired of hearing myself complain about this without actually doing anything about it. I decided to try six months of 'aggressive' online dating, meaning I forced myself to go on a new online date every week and a half or so during that time period. I went on about 16 first dates—not a single second date!—before I met my current boyfriend of three years. The whole thing was downright exhausting, but so totally worth it."

—LAUREN, 32, NEW YORK CITY

SETTING UP
A PROFILE

REMEMBER IN middle school and high school, when everyone used to send around those email chain-letters where you'd have to list your favorite color, your third-favorite book, the greatest memory from your childhood, etc., etc.? Well, filling out your profile is kind of like that but ultimately less pointless, because you get a date at the end. All you have to do is list your best, most flattering qualities. It's sort of a pleasant, ego-boosting way of spending fifteen to twenty minutes, when you think about it!

As is true for all good writing, *the more specific details, the better*. You want to paint a very clear picture of who you are. Sentences like "I'm a girl who likes to have fun" aren't very helpful: That you are a girl is (probably?) self-evident, and saying that you like to have fun doesn't really differentiate you from the rest of the population. How, specifically, do you like to have fun? What *kind* of a person are you? (Introverted, goofy, thoughtful, energetic, flirtatious, passionate, intellectual?) Each question on a dating profile is designed to help you showcase your specific personality. Yeah, some of them might be a bit dopey, but pointing this out in your answer doesn't actually do you any favors. (Answering a question with "Ask me in person ;-)," a surprisingly common occurrence, doesn't really entice the reader into messaging you to find out more.)

You also want to make sure that your profile makes you stand out from the other hundreds of profiles he's reading. List the hobbies, favorite movies, personality traits, and experiences that make you *you*. Arguably, in online dating, it's more important to seem compelling and interesting than it is to seem cool and aloof. Writing too much is better than writing too little.

But don't stress out about it, okay? Pour yourself a glass of wine and just write the first thing that comes to you. If you have fun filling out your profile, it will show in your answers—and that's a good thing. And no need to agonize over it for hours: The sooner you write a bang-up profile, the sooner you can get to the good stuff.

THE "ABOUT ME"

SELF-EXPRESSION and the ability to articulate your personality in a way that is appealing to someone else are an important part of dating, both online and off. Conveniently, your dating profile is a great way to practice this skill! Most dating sites, from OkCupid to FarmersOnly.com, have some sort of "About Me" section at the beginning of the profile, a blank space that you're supposed to fill with a clever and appealing self-summary. Pretty intimidating, actually, and way harder than simply filling out your favorite books. (We decided to skip the "About Me" section on HowAboutWe for this very reason: How can you *really* be expected to convey who you are in a paragraph? Other, more specific profile questions can be just as revealing.)

On sites that have an "About Me" section, don't let the blank space overwhelm you. What you're really doing here is giving the guy a teaser-trailer as to what it would be like to actually spend time with you. (*Teaser* means a SHORT paragraph or so, not a life history!) The best way to do this is to show instead of tell. List specific details that illustrate something about your personality, instead of just stating it.

For example:

❋ **Telling:** "I'm a fun-loving girl who's always up for trying new things."

❋ **Showing:** "I'm happiest when I'm catching a show at Webster Hall."

❋ **Telling:** "I'm extremely close to my family."

❋ **Showing:** "Sunday night means driving to see my parents, enjoying my mom's homemade spaghetti, and playing hide-and-seek with my nieces and nephews. My goal in life is to be their favorite aunt, so I try to visit and spoil them at least once a week."

❋ **Telling:** "I like to travel."

❋ **Showing:** "Last summer, I took a month off work and backpacked through South America. I slept in more train stations than I care to recall, climbed Machu Picchu at dawn, and completely ran out of money. Now I'm back in the States, recovering and saving money for my next great adventure . . . . "

THE PERFECT "ABOUT ME" FORMULA:

3 Hobbies + 2 Favorite Things + 1 Personality Descriptor

THE IMPORTANCE OF A KILLER PICTURE

YOUR PROFILE picture is the most important part of your online-dating profile. You can have the coolest hobbies in the world, the pithiest answers to the profile questions, and an "About Me" that makes the Gettysburg Address seem amateurish, but you're *still* not gonna get a second glance if your profile pic doesn't pass the test.

Yeah, it's shallow. But it's also human nature. A recent study by AnswerLab used an eye-tracker to see what part of a profile men actually spend the most time looking at, and wouldn't you know it? It's the profile picture.

So better open your tagged photos on Facebook and start looking for that killer shot. Obviously you want something flattering—a picture in which your hair looks great and you've managed to keep both eyes open and your outfit makes you look stylish and sexy. You also want a picture that looks recognizably like *you,* so nothing taken more than a year and a half ago. If it's a picture that you would consider using for a Facebook-profile picture, then it's a contender for a dating-profile picture.

But here's where dating-profile pictures and Facebook-profile pictures differ: Whereas on Facebook you might be tempted to put up a funny or goofy picture that shows off a more playful side of your personality, your dating picture should be fairly earnest. Unfortunately (and tough love here), men who are on dating sites tend to (unknowingly!) resort to more evolutionary tendencies. They're thinking "sex," they're looking for "sexy," and that picture of you with a fake mustache isn't going to cut it.

This is not to say that you need to book an appointment for a sultry photo shoot ASAP, but in general, you smiling naturally at the camera or looking relaxed in a candid shot is much sexier than you hamming it up with a donkey at the Grand Canyon. (You can keep the donkey picture! Just don't make it the *first* one he sees.) And, of course, happiness and confidence *are* sexy.

Once you've picked out a profile picture (or two), there's one final crucial step: Get a friend's opinion. You'd be surprised how often the pictures of ourselves that *we* like the best are *not* the same ones someone else would choose. Make sure they sign off on your choice before you publish your profile.

HOW MANY PHOTOS SHOULD YOU UPLOAD?

People with four photos get three times more messages than average.

$= 3 \times$ ✉

THE FIVE TYPES OF PICTURES EVERYONE SHOULD HAVE:

...AND FIVE TYPES TO AVOID:

1  The Super-Flattering Close-Up

1  The Mirror Self-Portrait

2  The "I Clean Up Nice" Shot from a Formal Event

2  The Cropped Photo of You and the Ex

3  The Action Shot

3  The Photo with Your Ridiculously, Distractingly Attractive Cousin

4  The "Oh, This Is Just Me Hanging Out at Machu Picchu" Vacation Shot

4  Photos of You with Babies or Small Children

5  The Mid-Laughter, Having Too Much Fun to Even Notice the Camera Shot

5  Any Photo with Duckface. (Just. Come on.)

TIP: Make sure that at least *one* of your photos is full-body. A selection of photos cropped close to the face will make the guy assume you're hiding something.

WHAT MAKES A PICTURE SUCCESSFUL?

W E TOOK A look at the main profile pictures of the five hundred most frequently messaged women on HowAboutWe to see if we could find any patterns. Are smiling photos more successful than not-smiling photos? Do blondes get the most clicks? It's hard to say how much of this is indicative of actual photo preference (versus, for example, a really funny profile or an awesome HowAboutWe date suggestion), but it seems that at the very least, uploading a profile picture in which you're smiling is never a bad idea. And please, please, please make sure people can get a good look at your face!

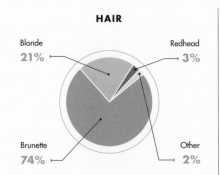

HAIR

Blonde
21%

Redhead
3%

Brunette
74%

Other
2%

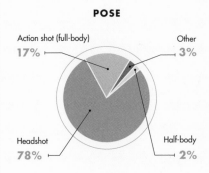

POSE

Action shot (full-body)
17%

Other
3%

Headshot
78%

Half-body
2%

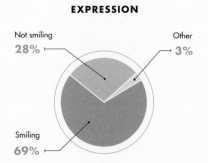

EXPRESSION

Not smiling
28%

Other
3%

Smiling
69%

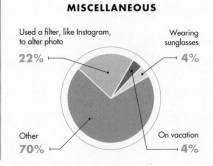

MISCELLANEOUS

Used a filter, like Instagram, to alter photo
22%

Wearing sunglasses
4%

Other
70%

On vacation
4%

———

O N ANY DATING SITE, the profile questions are carefully selected in order to make it easier to talk about yourself in an appealing, fun way. You don't have to answer every question, but the more you answer, the more chances you're giving a reader to like something about you.

Sure, the questions might seem a little goofy at times, but often the information revealed is surprisingly indicative of someone's personality. For example, let's take a look at some of HowAboutWe's profile questions. (Think of this as a sort of tutorial for when you're signing up for the three-month membership included in this book.)

1. "My Perfect Sunday"

If we were to ask about a Saturday night, everyone's answer would be similar ("out with friends!"). But talking about Sunday, the more low-pressure day of the weekend, gives you a chance to really show what kind of fun you like to have. Do you spend the day relaxing or going on an adventure? Are you religious? Social? Family-oriented? Do you make it a point to catch Sunday-night football?

The question asks about your *perfect* Sunday, so don't worry about being realistic. But think: If you were dating someone, how would you two ideally spend the day? Reading the paper in bed? Going out for an early-morning bike ride? Meeting friends for brunch? You want to find someone (and look

for someone!) who thinks that your Sunday sounds pretty appealing. (Conversely, someone who likes to wake up at 6 a.m. and hit antiques sales might not be the best match for someone who insists on sleeping in till two.)

2. "An Awesome Place I've Visited"

This question isn't really about how well-traveled you are, so don't worry about having a "cool" answer. An awesome place could be your grandparents' farm in Idaho, or a hidden corner of the park in your city. The point is to give you a chance to describe somewhere that's special to you.

When answering the question, don't just say what the place was. Explain specifically *why* you were there, and *why* you thought it was great. What is it about this particular place that stands out above others in your mind?

3. "I Want to Come Home to . . . "

Do you and your potential date/boyfriend/husband/partner have the same idea of domestic bliss? If all long-term relationships eventually lead to some sort of domesticity (whether it's living together or just spending a lot of time together), then it's not always going to be about what to do when you're out. This is a chance to give a taste of what you're looking for on the homefront.

So think of it this way: You've just finished a long and exhausting day, and you're finally getting home. What's on the other side of that front door? A martini? A guy who makes you laugh? Chinese takeout and DVR-ed sitcoms? A warm bath? A newly made bed? Kids who are excited to see you? Describe your idea of home, so that whoever is reading your profile can try to imagine himself in it.

4. "Obscure Knowledge I Possess"

Everyone retains some trivial information in her brain; the *type* of trivial information is hugely telling. The person who remembers every minor Star Wars character is different from the person who can tell you how to resuscitate a blue warbler, who is different from the person who can list the Tudor line of succession.

Remember, how you *got* that useless information is often more interesting than the information itself, so mention that in your answer, too.

5. "If I Won the Lottery and Quit My Job, I Would . . . "

Your job doesn't define you, so this question gets rid of that restriction and tries to get to the heart of who you really are, based on what you'd do if you had no responsibilities.

Would you travel the world? Would you write a novel? Give the money away? Buy a library and live in it? Buy a soccer team? Or not quit your job at all, because you love what you're currently doing?

DRINKING AND EXERCISE

Here's something interesting: If you're a woman and you say you drink a lot, you get double the messages of men who say they drink a lot. Turns out that women are much more turned off by heavy drinking than men. However, women who say they drink a moderate amount get more messages than those who say they drink a lot. Women who say they never drink get significantly fewer messages. Exercise is pretty predictable: Women who say they exercise "often" or "a lot" get the most messages.

PROFILES: *The Good and the Bad*

	WHAT YOU SHOULDN'T DO
1	Head shots give very little sense of what the person actually looks like—at least one full-body is a must!
2	This date is a little vague. Why not name a specific bar or cocktail to try?
3	Not very specific or interesting!
4	Boring!
5	Again, very vague. Doesn't give a real sense of what she's like, apart from where she's lived. Absolutely no indication of what it would be like to actually hang out with this girl.
6	Cliché answer!
7	This girl probably isn't very good at telling funny stories . . . or holding an interesting conversation . . . .
8	Oh, boy!

CGA625

26, Female, Straight
San Francisco, CA

HOW ABOUT WE...
get to know each other
over a cocktail?

PHOTOS

Career:
Start-up

Education:
College

Height:
5'5"

How much do you exercise?

Never   Often

How much do you drink?

Never   Often

ABOUT CGA625

An Awesome Place I've Visited:
Rome, Italy

My Perfect Sunday:
Having a few beers and getting some work done.

My Life History in 5 Sentences or Fewer:
Grew up in SoCal, college in L.A., moved to San Fran for work. I'm passionate about music, reading, and the environment.

My First Concert:
No Doubt

I Have a Weakness for Guys With:
Nice eyes.

A Story You Should Remind Me to Tell You on Our First Date:
My crazy college roommate.

1

2

3

4

5

6

7

8

(2)

LemonToast **(3) → name pointer**

26, Female, Straight

San Francisco, CA

(1)

> **HOW ABOUT WE...**
> check out the earthquake exhibit at the San Francisco Aquarium, then head to a bar for some fortifying whiskey?

(3)

PHOTOS

Career:
Start-up

Education:
College

Height:
5'5"

How much do you exercise?

Never   Often

(8)

How much do you drink?

Never   Often

ABOUT LemonToast

(4)

An Awesome Place I Visited:
Rome, Italy—I spent three weeks there as part of a photojournalism class in college. Best field trip I've ever been on . . . .

My Perfect Sunday:
Grab the paper and a croissant from my favorite neighborhood café, go for a run, meet friends for a late brunch, maybe catch a movie in the afternoon, cook a big meal (usually my signature spaghetti carbonara), and hopefully be on the couch in front of the TV in time for *Mad Men*.

(5)

An Infatuation of Mine:
I collect coffee mugs from diners, but only if they have the name of the diner printed on it. Road trips have proven to be a pretty good way of expanding the collection.

(6)

I Have a Weakness for Guys Who:
Have dogs! I know it's a cliché, but something about a guy playing with a dog just gets me.

A Story You Should Remind Me to Tell You on Our First Date:
The time I got the date of my friend's wedding wrong . . . which I basically only discovered once I saw the wrong bride walking down the aisle. And then I just stayed for the whole ceremony, 'cause at that point it seemed rude to leave? And then I got stuck in the receiving line.

(7)

WHAT YOU SHOULD DO

1   This girl looks happy and confident in all her photos. They're flattering and also give a good snapshot of what her life might be like.

2   No idea what this profile name means, but it's caught our attention.

3   Listing multiple dates is smart: If someone isn't interested in one date, you suggest he might be interested in a different one.

4   She sounds interesting, and there's already something a guy can comment on or ask her about.

5   Anyone reading this can already picture what spending a weekend with her might be like, and she's given us a lot of information about herself in just a few lines. (She cooks, she works out, she's social, she watches TV, etc.)

6   Random and distinctive—an easy conversation-starter for any guy reading her profile and looking for something to talk to her about. ("What's the coolest mug you have?" "What was the best road trip you've taken so far?" etc.)

7   This story already seems funny and cute, and it definitely makes you want to hear her tell it in person.

8   All right, so she probably drinks more than that. But she's not going to give it away in her profile. Very measured, average responses, in terms of drinking/exercise.

ARE YOU BEING HONEST ENOUGH ON YOUR PROFILE?

☒ *Before you click "publish" on that profile, ask yourself . . .*

☐ 1. Are the hobbies listed on your profile your *actual* hobbies?

☐ 2. Is your profile picture representative of what you *actually* look like?

☐ 3. Do you say you're open to something casual when you really just want a serious boyfriend, or vice versa?

OKAY, BUT HOW HONEST DO YOU HAVE TO BE, *REALLY*?

Filling out a dating profile honestly is a tricky thing. On the one hand, you don't want to misrepresent yourself, if only because ultimately that will bring you incompatible matches. But on the other hand, there is such a thing as *too* honest. You spend most of your Friday evenings happily eating chicken tikka masala in bed and watching reality shows about weddings, but you probably don't want to advertise it on your profile.

Bending the truth a *little* isn't necessarily a bad thing when filling out your profile, especially when you realize that people do the exact same thing when meeting in person. It's totally natural to overemphasize or exaggerate certain hobbies or interests when you first meet someone in the hopes of seeming more compatible. (I've definitely told guys that I LOVE a certain TV show when, in reality, I've maybe caught three or four episodes in my lifetime.)

Example, one girl I talked to said that though she's super-outdoorsy and loves hiking, camping, etc., she stopped listing that on her dating profile because she found she was attracting only a very specific type of guy, and every single date was a hiking date. Not mentioning her love of the outdoors on her profile doesn't mean she lied about her interests or stopped doing nature-related things with guys once they started dating; she just slightly altered the focus of the first impression she was making.

So a little poetic license is okay. Just make sure that whatever you claim has more truth to it than falsehood. Exaggerating an interest is fine; completely making one up is not.

THINGS PEOPLE BEND THE TRUTH ABOUT ON THEIR PROFILES

These little white lies from anonymous HowAboutWe daters are ultimately pretty forgiveable, but just remember: You get what you ask for. So if you're going to say you love the outdoors, you'd better be ready to break out your hiking shoes.

1. "That I don't watch TV (I totally watch TV)."

2. "I definitely omit some of my more embarrassing music tastes."

3. "I try to sound more positive than I actually am."

4. "Drug usage. There's no way to say I smoke pot without sounding like a stoner."

5. "I say I drink less than I do."

6. "I overemphasize my outdoorsy-ness."

7. "That I'm 'up for anything'— no, not on a weeknight."

8. "Taste in movies. Let's be real— it's mostly chick flicks, but that doesn't get guys going.'"

9. "I say I'm 5'8"—I'm 5'5", but I wear a lot of heels and wedges."

10. "How much I like sports (I actually like them more than I say I do)."

MEETING
and
MESSAGING

S O THE SECOND you sign up for online dating, you'll probably get a fair amount of creepy/uncouth/uninteresting messages from guys whom you have absolutely no interest in dating. These gentlemen will message hundreds of women in one sitting—they hardly dare expect a response, and you certainly don't have to feel obligated to give them one.

The *most* annoying thing about these guys (apart from the staggering lack of creativity in their messages) is that they are so vociferous that they sometimes drown out the guys who are actually worth talking to. *But that doesn't mean the guys worth talking to aren't there.*

It simply means that when it comes to online dating, it's better for girls to message guys. The worst thing you can do is just fill out a profile and wait for Prince Charming to message you out of the blue. Better take matters into your own hands and message a few potential Prince Charmings yourself.

Something else to keep in mind: People who are good at online dating (at How-AboutWe, we call them "superusers") will message people *a lot*. I mean, that's the point, right? To meet as many potential dates as possible? So don't message only one guy and then wait for his response. Get a lot of conversations started so that you don't put too much weight on one exchange. The more irons in the fire, the more potential dates to choose from.

HOW TO MESSAGE SOMEONE

1. Don't "introduce" yourself.
That's way too formal for online dating! Just launch right into your opener—the more relaxed and conversational, the better.

"Nice North Carolina gear! I moved here from NC a few years ago. Are you a Tar Heel fan, too?"

2. Respond to something in his profile.
You'll have plenty of time in later messages to talk about yourself, so don't worry about launching into a biography. The first message is just the icebreaker—mention something in his profile so that he knows you read it (and that you don't just think he's hot).

"Pretty cool that you're into geography—I'm a huge fan of maps and I personally think the iPhone is really taking all the fun out of road trips. Hope your week has been good so far."

3. Keep it short, and end with a question.
Don't write more than a few sentences for your opening message. Make it easy and quick to read. Last, give him something to actually respond to, so that it's easy for him to dash off a quick message back.

"Love Ender's Game! *Have you read the other books in the series?"*

4. If the guy has "winked" at you or sent you an "I'm Intrigued" . . .
He wants to let you know he likes you but is too shy to write an actual message (or he doesn't know what to say!). This means it's up to you to start up a conversation. You know he's already into you, so just keep it simple!

"Hi! So I'm new to this and I'm not too sure what the next step is, but I guess we're both 'intrigued'? ha. How long have you lived in Chicago? Claire"

5. If you wait a really long time to respond . . .
Maybe you were seeing someone, or just really busy. It's totally worth sending someone a message a few weeks, or even months, after he reached out to you. Just apologize for the delay, and don't be too upset if he's no longer interested.

"Hey, Joe! Sorry I haven't written back—I took a break from the site for a while. If you're still up for it, I'd love to grab a drink sometime and swap travel stories."

6. If he's hot but hasn't answered enough profile questions . . .
He's giving you absolutely nothing to go off of, but he's hot enough for you to still be interested. Send him a message inviting him to tell you more about himself—it doesn't matter how inane your question might be.

"You're definitely attractive, but I'd like to know more. What do you do? Seen any good movies lately?"

WHEN TO PROPOSE A DATE
AND HOW TO DO IT

HAVING CHEMISTRY online does *not* mean you'll have chemistry offline, and the best way to ensure that you're not just wasting your time is to meet the guy in person. Don't spend weeks composing long epistles to a guy you've never met; that allows you to create a version of this person in your mind that he is almost guaranteed not to live up to. In other words, you're kind of sabotaging a chance at the real thing. If after a few back-and-forths you've ascertained that he's as likable as he seems on his profile, suggest meeting in person. You can chat on the phone before you meet, but it's probably better to just risk twenty-five minutes over a cup of coffee and see how you connect face-to-face. Then you'll have a much better idea of whether or not this is someone you *actually* want to date. If not, move on to the next guy!

Here's what to say:

❋ **"A new tapas place just opened up in my neighborhood. Let me know if you'd be interested in checking it out with me."**

❋ **"You! Wanna grab a drink sometime? Your 'Perfect Sunday' won me over."**

❋ **"I'd love to grab coffee and get to know you in person . . . Are you around next Tuesday after work? There's a great place in Brooklyn that serves the best espresso."**

DON'T WINK

The "Wink" or "Flirt" feature on online-dating sites is basically useless. It just throws the ball into the other person's court without giving him or her anything to respond to. It's always more effective to just write a message!

ONLINE-DATING FAQS

❋ **What if you see someone you know on the site?**
You have three options: a) Stalk him, b) Send him a cheeky "wink" or message as a joke, or c) Ignore it and pretend you never saw it.

❋ **Should you sign your real name?**
First name, definitely! Last name, only if you're okay with being Google-searched.

❋ **What if you lose interest?**
No big deal. Just say, "Hey, you seem great, and I've enjoyed talking to you, but I didn't feel a connection. Good luck with your search!"

❋ **What if he loses interest?**
Whatever! On to the next profile. Don't get too discouraged: You want to find the person who really wants to find you.

❋ **What if you go on a date with someone and then see him again on the site?**
Most sites let you block users. Otherwise, don't worry too much about it. You're both just looking for another date.

❋ **When should you take your profile down after seeing someone?**
Only once you've decided to be exclusive—but you have to have had the conversation!

❋ **Is it dishonest to send many people the same message?**
It's not the end of the world, though personalized messages will probably get a better response rate. But only the first message. Once you start an exchange with someone, no more copying and pasting!

❋ **If I have a disability, do I have an obligation to list it on my profile?**
You aren't obliged to list it on your profile, but you should probably give him a heads-up before you meet in person.

❋ **If I have a kid, do I have an obligation to list that on my profile?**
No, but do mention it *very* early on in your messages.

❋ **Only gross guys are messaging me.**
If you aren't happy with the messages you're receiving, focus on the messages you're sending to guys!

HE STILL HAS AN ONLINE-DATING PROFILE

"I met a guy on an online-dating site, and things have been going really well. After our first date over a month ago, we've seen each other regularly (about once a week), we've slept together, and I really get the impression that this is something special for both of us. I haven't used the dating site since our first date, but I randomly signed on about a week ago and saw that he was also "currently online." I've checked up on him since—I know, bad—and he seems to be still using the site pretty actively. Is this weird, or do guys on dating sites just date around a lot?"

—ANONYMOUS, 35, LOS ANGELES

Have you guys decided to see each other exclusively? If not, then he's totally within his right to continue to actively use the site—and so are you! If you aren't comfortable with the idea of his going on other dates (and it seems like you aren't), then it's time to have a serious conversation about your relationship expectations.

But just to explore another possibility for a moment: Just because he is logging in to his site doesn't mean that he's actively dating on it. He could be signing in to read a random message, or to see if you're signing in. And some people keep a profile up—however inactive—even when they are dating someone. If you're boyfriend and girlfriend and he's still logging in to the site every day, then that's weird, but until you're at that point, it's pretty normal for someone to keep his options somewhat open during the early stages of dating.

DATING-PROFILE DECODER

❉ If he messages you and just says, "Hey," but nothing else . . . **he's messaging a thousand other people. Literally a thousand.**

❉ If he messages you after midnight on a weekend . . . **he either has no friends or is very drunk. Quite possibly both.**

❉ If he writes, "I love to have fun!" on his profile . . . **he probably isn't nearly as fun-loving as he claims to be.**

❉ If he claims he doesn't know what to say about himself . . . **he lacks confidence and creativity.**

❉ If he claims it's his first time dating online, or he "doesn't usually do stuff like this" . . . **he's still insecure about online dating, and maybe not fully committed yet.**

❉ If he lists "working out" or "going to the gym" as a hobby or interest . . . **he thinks of himself as fit and wants you to be too.**

❉ If he talks about sex in his profile . . . **he's probably looking for something more akin to a casual encounter than a relationship.**

❉ If he lists *To Kill a Mockingbird* or *The Great Gatsby* as his favorite book, with no other examples . . . **there's a good chance he hasn't read a book since high school.**

❉ If he starts off his profile with a long list of things he doesn't want in someone . . . **he's negative and defensive. On to the next profile!**

❉ If he has a dog or a baby in his profile picture . . . **give him props for really pulling out all the stops.**

❉ If his profile is completely sarcastic and glib . . . **he hasn't let his guard down. Proceed with caution.**

LESBIANS AND ONLINE DATING

I F YOU'RE a lesbian, you're crazy not to online-date. The scene is so small that it's to your utmost advantage to use all the tools at your disposal to meet people. Women who aren't necessarily out, women who frequent a different gay bar, or women who maybe just live in a slightly different neighborhood: You have a much better chance of meeting them online than anywhere else. And don't worry about getting hit on by guys: Most dating sites (HowAboutWe included) won't show your profile to anyone other than the gender that *you're* interested in. It's a totally safe (and effective!) dating environment. Again, online dating shouldn't necessarily be the *only* way you meet women, but between dating sites and Ladies Night you should be able to get a fairly well-rounded dating pool.

Regarding setting up your profile, all the rules previously discussed in this chapter apply: Choose at least three flattering photographs, including a full-body shot and one that clearly shows your face. If you identify strongly with a certain gender role or characteristics (e.g., femme, butch, lipstick), you want to make that clear on your profile. If a picture won't actively convey this, then drop hints (or flat-out *say* it) in the profile itself (lest you meet and discover you're not attracted to each other).

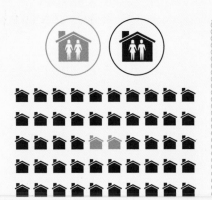

In 2012, Northampton, Massachusetts, had more lesbians per capita than any other town or city in the country.

There were about forty same-sex couples per 1,000 households there.*

*about 2 out of 50

HOW TO DATE ONLINE

W HEN IT comes to online dating, deciding to sign up isn't the hard part. Filling out a profile or sending a first message isn't the hard part. The hard part is actually *dating,* and that doesn't take place online at all. And (not to equate your love life with being on a football team or anything) dating takes patience, commitment, and stamina.

A dating site isn't a miracle solution; it's just an efficient way of meeting people. You're still going to have to sift through the eligible bachelors and perhaps suffer through some less-than-amazing dates before you find the right guy. But don't get too discouraged! A few lackluster dates are just par for the course. If you give up on the whole idea of online dating after just one or two disappointments, then you haven't really used the site to your best advantage.

If you're going to put all that work and effort into setting up an online-dating profile, you might as will give it a real shot. Give yourself a window of time (six months is a good amount, but even three will do), and try to actively use the site during that period. This means logging on, seeking people out, messaging, and, yes, going on dates. If you've had a profile for six months but only gone on three dates, you haven't *really* done online dating; you've just sort of halfheartedly tried it.

Yes, it's a lot of effort. But if you're at a point in your life where you're serious about finding someone, then it's going to take effort.

Of course staying in and watching a movie is easier than making small talk with a complete stranger. Of course grabbing a drink with your friends is a safer bet. Of course risking rejection or awkwardness or an unpleasant time is way more work than just . . . not bothering.

But if you make a serious attempt at this, and if you will yourself to suffer through the mediocrity, then all the effort and dates will eventually seem worth it. Use your How-AboutWe membership, go on some awesome dates, meet new people, and see where it takes you. There's someone great out there for you. You just might have to go on lots of first dates to find him.

In 2012, a third of America's 90 million singles were dating online—

not counting those who hooked up through Facebook and other social-media sites.

Chapter 4

FIRST DATES

THE BASICS

Sweet! You have a date. First dates are so exciting!
And also scary. But mostly exciting!

THE CRAZIEST THING, I think, about first dates is that each first date has the possibility of being your *last* first date. This date could be the one that you recall fondly for years to come—how you couldn't find the restaurant, how he was wearing a pink shirt, how you both decided to take a walk after dinner and ended up walking for hours until you realized it was 2 a.m. and you both had work the next morning. How you actually started grinning *during* the first kiss, because it was just too perfect. How the next day you woke up at seven and couldn't wait for your best friend to call, text, or email so that you could tell her *everything*. How you managed to tell her, coolly, "Well, we'll see how it goes," as if you weren't letting yourself get too excited, as if you didn't absolutely *know* in your bones that it was the beginning of something exciting, of something important in your life.

Of course, not all first dates are like that.

There are also the bad first dates. These play out like endurance tests: How much awkwardness can you possibly withstand in the course of a two-hour meal, a forty-five-minute drink, a painful thirty-minute cup of coffee? Dates where you discover, to your horror, that you actually *loathe* the person sitting next to you. Dates where you find yourself running to the bathroom to text frantic "WTF"s to your friend and furtively scanning the room for hidden cameras, because it has to be a joke, right? This guy has to actually be a joke. And then,

I knew what I wanted in a guy.
Manners. Napkin on the lap.
Being considerate of the waitstaff."

—Briana, 25, Chicago

finally, you make your escape. Relief floods your entire body. Your fingers shake as you eagerly dial your friend's number: She's not going to *believe* this. You smile to yourself as you get into bed that night, out of the sheer joy of knowing that you survived, that you are *never* seeing that guy again. As early as the next day, you get a certain amount of pleasure from telling people the story. You become a kind of raconteur with it, and eventually you know which parts to skip and which parts to highlight in order to elicit the best reactions when you tell it. For years and years to come, it's one of your most reliably entertaining anecdotes.

Then there are the dates that are perfectly fine. The dates where you have an okay conversation, an okay dinner, an okay time. The

nights where you shake hands or hug at the end of the night, and maybe walk home feeling a teensy bit despondent. Your friend will text you "???" and you'll respond, "Meh," and maybe you'll give him another shot, and maybe you won't. These dates aren't horrible, but they're definitely not the best.

It's like playing the lottery; you never know what you're going to get. A pleasant conversation? A hilarious story? A movie that you wanted to see anyway? A pretty satisfying make-out session? A new friend? Or that glimmering possibility that comes with every exchange of phone numbers or casual "Wanna get a drink sometime?" email: Will this be *the* date that you'll one day look back on as the beginning?

HOW TO PLAN (NEARLY) FOOLPROOF DATES

T HE POINT OF A DATE is to determine whether you have any romantic chemistry. But chemistry is something that develops when both people are feeling super-relaxed and comfortable enough to actively engage with one another— and on first dates, it's *hard* to immediately feel relaxed, especially if you're out with someone you don't know very well. You end up staring at the cocktail menu for an unnecessarily long time, just to buy yourself some time to think of something to say.

So here's the trick: **If you want to get both people feeling at ease, give the date a secondary focus.** It can be an activity you're going to do, a game you're going to watch, or a food item or drink you're going to try. This allows you both to feel like you're there for an express purpose *other* than just sizing each other up for romantic potential. Instead of having to rack your brain to think of conversation topics, conversation will move along quite naturally with the activity at hand.

This is why classes, museum exhibits, or physically active dates are often so successful: Both people are engaged in the activity and can sort of forget about being on a date and start having fun with each other. And you're *so* much more likely to actually *like* someone when you're doing something fun, or silly, or kind of difficult, rather than just interviewing each other over beers.

So when it comes time to plan your date, whatever base *type* of setting or activity you choose, make sure to add in some sort of other layer so that you'll have something to do and talk about. Instead of meeting for drinks, find a bar with pool or darts or Big Buck Hunter. Instead of just meeting for dinner, try to find a specific restaurant or weird menu item that you both want to try.

Once you have a secondary focus, you'll find that any number of activities and settings can make a good first date, depending on what qualities or characteristics you're going for.

THE BEST TIMES TO ASK SOMEONE OUT

IF SITE TRAFFIC from online-dating sites is any indication (and obviously it is), then Tuesday seems to be the day that most people, having fully recovered from their weekends, fire up the old computer and see what the romantic possibilities are.

In other words, the weekend is not a good time to ask someone out, even if you're planning ahead for *next* week. People just aren't at their computers/by their phones all the time on weekends; they're out having fun, and frankly, you should be, too! (Besides, as we discussed in Chapter 2, an important part of dating is being happy, an important part of being happy is having a social life, and even if *you* know that you were perfectly content

spending Saturday night in a face mask, watching *Sherlock*, and falling into a deep, restful sleep at 9 p.m., you don't exactly want to advertise that fact by choosing Saturday night to message someone.) Do your date planning at the beginning of the week.

Because people have such busy schedules, it's probably safest to plan dates about five days in advance. Shorter notice works sometimes, especially if you have something pop up, like concert tickets or an event of some sort. Spontaneity works if it's someone you already have some sort of relationship with, but most "Hey, what are you doing tonight?" texts imply boredom or booty call, even if that isn't actually your intent.

71% of daters surveyed by HowAboutWe.com said

they've never stood someone up.

The Types of FIRST DATES

DRINK DATES

Pros: Alcohol = conversational lubrication. More romantic than coffee but less of a commitment than dinner. Easy to prolong or cut short after one drink, depending.

Cons: Not everyone drinks! Can be hard to think of things to talk about if there's no immediate chemistry. The worry of drinking *too much*.

SOBER DATES

Pros: No need to worry about beer goggles or whether you're acting a little too, shall we say, ebullient. You can be sure your judgement isn't impaired.

Cons: They don't call alcohol a social lubricant for nothing! A bar, whether it's a wine bar or a dive bar, can also just be a nice place to hang out after dark, and bars tend to stay open later than coffee shops.

ACTIVITY DATES

Pros: Gets you both out of your element, on the same team. Easy icebreaker. Can focus on *doing* something rather than asking the usual "date-y" questions. See what it's like to actually hang out with someone, rather than just drink with him.

Cons: If the date isn't good, you're still stuck doing whatever activity with him. People can feel *too* much out of their element.

SHOPPING DATES

Pros: A quick way to get to know a person's taste/ shared aesthetic sensibility. A shared "mission," if you're shopping for something in particular. Fun and easy to discuss weird or cool finds.

Cons: Just walking around and looking at stuff can get a little boring. Can be hard to segue the conversation into other things *besides* the immediate present. And *definitely* not a good date for people who don't like to browse or shop!

LISTEN OR WATCH DATES

Pros: A movie or a concert is a great way to explore a shared interest. It's also a nice way to kill two birds with one stone, if there's a concert or a movie you particularly want to go to. Experiencing an amazing show together can be a bonding experience, and it gives you plenty of fodder for conversation when it's over.

Cons: A movie or a show certainly isn't a great way to get to *know* someone, seeing as you're basically greeting each other and then focusing all your attention on whatever entertainment's at hand. So it might be a little awkward, and further icebreakers may be necessary!

COFFEE DATES

Pros: The best, most low-pressure scenario for dates that you're feeling "iffy" about. Daytime coffee entails virtually no pressure to extend the date past an hour, though of course it's easy to do so if there's a spark. The fact that a cup of coffee is inexpensive is another bonus.

Cons: Well, it's certainly not romantic. You'd be hard-pressed to have a coffee date end in a first kiss, unless you either move on to drinks/dinner/another activity or stay there for *hours*. But who, apart from freelancers and students, wants to stay at a coffee shop for *hours*?

EXPLORE DATES

Pros: The thrill of discovering a new neighborhood, coffee shop or art gallery can be a great way to bond. The cheesy lines practically write themselves: "We'll always have GOWANUS . . . ."

Cons: Exploring can be fun, but aimlessly walking around can get a little tiring, especially if the place you're exploring doesn't turn out to be that . . . interesting. If things on the date don't go well, it's a *loooong* trip back to where you started.

VOLUNTEER DATES

Pros: You'll feel virtuous and you'll get to know each other while actually making a difference. You'll instantly have something to do—it's sort of like an activity date with added karma. And you'll totally have earned a post-volunteering drink! (Or three.)

Cons: Depending on the task, volunteering can be emotionally taxing. That can be some pretty heavy stuff to experience with someone you've just met.

THE TRAITS OF A PERFECT FIRST-DATE SPOT

THE PERSON YOU'RE with is obviously the most important factor in whether or not a date will be enjoyable, but the location and ambiance play a major part too. A bad first-date setting can fizzle any potential chemistry almost immediately, especially if either of you is distracted by environmental factors or situational awkwardness. Conversely, an amazing, fun, and relaxed date setup can be all it takes for you to see a guy you were feeling iffy about in a whole new, romantic light . . . .

1. It's somewhere you like but not your favorite spot.

Your favorite spot is sacred, man. Don't take someone there unless you've pre-vetted him and know you'll have a good time. Save it for the third or fourth date.

2. It's someplace you can chill for up to two hours.

If your date goes well, you're going to end up lingering a long time, even if you were just meeting for coffee. Choose an environment where you can really relax and not even notice how much time has gone by.

3. It's close to other things.

Always have a plan for how to elongate the date if it goes well. For example: If you meet up for coffee, make sure there's a restaurant nearby in case you want to suggest dinner. If you've met up for dinner, choose someplace that's near a bar where you could go for a nightcap.

4. It's not too loud.

Nothing kills potential romance like having to scream, "What??" to each other over and over again.

5. It's far enough away from where you live.

It's okay to hope that the evening ends up at your place. But you have to at least *pretend* that you weren't planning on ending up there all along. Choose somewhere that's at least a few blocks away—picking someplace across the street is poor form. (Not that I haven't fallen for it.)

6. It's lively enough.

It can be surprisingly uncomfortable to have a first date at a bar or a restaurant where you're the only patrons. Having other people around can go a long way toward making things feel more natural, and discussing the people around you is always a good talking point if the conversation runs dry.

7. **It's not your "Cheers" bar.**
If you're lucky enough to have a bar where everyone truly knows your name (in 2012, no less!), then you should feel pretty badass, but you should not choose this spot for first dates. Way too intimidating for your date! On a first date, you want someplace where the chances of running into someone you know (and awkwardly having to introduce your date as . . . a friend? And possibly having to small-talk with the interloper . . .) are slim.

THE WORST SIX WORDS TO SAY ON A DATE

I F YOU WANT to be a good dater (and a good person!), you will eliminate as much of the "planning" work for your date as possible, or at least facilitate fast and easy decisions once you're actually on the date. Because round after round of "What do you want to do?" "I dunno, what do *you* want to do?" "I'm fine with whatever." "So what should we do?" is soul-sucking and demoralizing and will end with one or both people fervently wishing they had just stayed home and read a book. To avoid this scenario, make sure to:

1. **Show up with a plan.**

2. **Have a backup plan.**

3. **Present options instead of a vague, open-ended question.**

4. **If your date says, "I don't care" (damn him!), then just make a decision yourself.**

The
PRE-DATE RITUAL

THE HOUR, or two hours, or twenty minutes you spend getting ready for a date is actually a pretty important part of the process. It's when you psych yourself up, try to deal with nerves, spend more time on your eye makeup than usual, moisturize, call your best friend for reassurance, try to take a picture of your outfit, have a glass of wine, change your outfit, look in the mirror, double-check the address on Google Maps, spritz perfume, look in the mirror one last time, and pronounce yourself Ready for This Date.

Rushing to a date immediately after work is certainly doable, and often a necessity. But there's something so nice about getting to spend time preparing for a date. You arrive feeling focused, ready, and more confident about how you look than if you'd just rushed in from work.

And it's *fun*. There's a reason so many movies have corny "girls getting ready" montages—sitting in front of the mirror putting on makeup and blasting music is, like, a rite of passage. Whatever your personal pre-date ritual is (and it really can be anything), use the time to relax, to feel good about yourself, and to get excited. You're starring in your own personal movie (romantic comedy? tragedy? tragi-comedy? depends on the date!), so enjoy it.

FIVE TIPS FOR PRE-DATE PREPPING

LEANDRA MEDINE, *Founder, ManRepeller.com*

---

1. **Buying a new outfit for a date isn't always a great idea.**
There's something to be said about that novel, fleeting moment that only a new garment can provide, but generally I have found it's best to stick with what you know/ have in matters of the date. The novel, fleeting moment in this case shouldn't come from your clothes.

2. **If he's overly focused on your outfit, he's probably not worth it anyway.**
It's not really a matter of a dude getting your outfit or not, and the fact of the matter is, if that's a deal-breaker on a date, you're more or less lucky you've found out how hard he sucks this early.

3. **Always wear something comfortable and preferably not too tight.**
Steer away from shoes you can't walk in and dresses so tight that the composition of the birthmarks on your ass is practically transparent.

4. **Remember to psych yourself up. It sounds cheesy, but it totally works.**
Think about when you feel best about yourself. Do what it takes to get there before your date.

5. **Dress for you, not for him.**
The art of a date outfit is much more about a woman's internalized sense of self. If you feel great, you will be great.

43% of daters suveyed said

Google-searching their date is part of their pre-date ritual.

TEN THINGS TO HAVE IN YOUR PURSE
ON A FIRST DATE

1. **Tissues**

2. **Deodorant**
(hopefully you won't need to use it, but oh my God, if you need to you will be so happy you brought it along, so you're not, like, trying to wash with paper towels in the bathroom.)

3. **Mints or gum**
(for you to use or casually offer)

4. **Cash**
(enough to pay for your portion and get a cab home)

5. **The very basic things you personally feel you need in order to feel pretty**
(such as mascara, lip gloss)

6. **Lip balm**

7. **A book. A pack of cards. Something that can double as a conversation starter and something to entertain yourself with.**

8. **Phone charger**
(Because there is nothing worse than running late, or not being able to find the restaurant, and having your phone die)

9. **Condoms**
(just in case!)

10. **Meds**
(birth control, allergy medicine, whatever you might need in case you spend the night)

HIT UP THE ATM BEFORE YOUR DATE

Always go to a date prepared to pay for at least your portion of the bill. Cash is the safest bet, as (infuriatingly!) not every place accepts cards. If you do put down a card (at a bar, for instance), the bill is inexpensive, you think you want to go out with the person again, and you can afford it, consider just footing the bill. It's generous, sexy, and less awkward than accepting cash from him like your date was a transaction.

I PURPOSELY WEAR UGLY UNDERWEAR ON A FIRST DATE

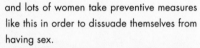

"Is it weird to have first-date panties
(ugly ones, so that you won't sleep with him no matter what)?"

—AUDREY, 24, BROOKLYN

Is it weird? Not weird—pretty common, actually. Other variations include not shaving/waxing (pubic hair as a chastity belt!) and, conversely, women resigning themselves to not having sex (even if they'd like to) while wearing Spanx. It's not weird because lots

and lots of women take preventive measures like this in order to dissuade themselves from having sex.

But just so we're clear, it's *you* who cares about the ugly underwear. You get that, right? A guy who is about to get laid is not concerned with whether you're wearing La Perla or the elastic-less Hanes you've had since the tenth grade. Old underwear (or pubic hair, or Spanx) is simply not a deterrent for a guy who is about to have sex.

If you, for whatever reason, have decided you do not want to be tempted into having sex, and you feel like your choice of underwear will affect how you feel about the prospect of taking off your clothes, then it seems like a relatively effective insurance policy. But in general, we're pro wearing clothes that make you feel confident and sexy on first dates, not unfuckable.

HOW TO DEAL WITH FIRST-DATE JITTERS

I GET REALLY nervous before first dates. So nervous, in fact, that I've never had a first date that I didn't seriously consider canceling the day of. Strange, considering that a) I make my living pumping other people up about dating; b) I don't experience any other type of social anxiety; and, most poignantly, c) I've never had a *bad* date. Sure, I've had "eh" dates, but I've never left a date thinking, *That was awful and miserable and uncomfortable.*

Why all the nerves, then, when I have ample evidence that dates always turn out okay and, at the very least, always end? I couldn't tell you. All I know is that the buildup to every first date has me calling my mother/all my female friends, looking for someone, *anyone,* to validate me in my thinking that he totally won't mind if I just call it off twenty minutes before. ("GO ON THE DAMN DATE" is the universal response.)

Meeting a near-stranger in order to mutually assess your romantic compatibility is a really intimidating prospect. Unfortunately, I've found that the only thing that really elim-

inates pre-date jitters (*pre-date dread* might be a more apt term, actually) is to just go on the date. The second the date starts, my nerves are quelled. It really is the anticipation that's the worst part. Once the date is happening, I'm able to see it for what it really is: a casual, low-stakes opportunity to get to know someone and not, say, an excruciatingly awkward social encounter that will forever determine my prospects of future happiness/the fate of mankind. (*I know*, but you should see me before dates.)

The other thing that helps with eliminating nervousness before dates is simply going on a lot of dates. It does get a little better each time you go through the cycle. Fractionally better, maybe, but better. And if you schedule multiple dates with different guys over, say, a two-week period, you'll feel proportionately less stressed out about each individual one.

I guess the point here is that you might not be able to eliminate pre-date jitters from your life, but you can cope with them. Try the tricks on the following pages.

HOW TO STAY CALM
BEFORE A DATE

Possibly out of Darwinian necessity, women have adapted various strategies for dealing with nerves before a first date. Guaranteed to eliminate (or at least reduce?) the terror!

"I don't know how brilliant/unique this is, but I always try to tell myself that I'm just meeting a friend, to take all the romantic pressure off. Low expectations!"

—MEREDITH, 28, WASHINGTON, D.C.

"Make plans for immediately *after* the date, thus setting a time cap. It's easier to face the prospect of a date when you know that no matter what, at X p.m. you have to leave and go do something else. If the date goes really well, you'll look extra-forward to the next time."

—CHIARA, 26, NEW YORK CITY
(author of this book; expert at being nervous before dates)

"I have a friend come over while I'm getting ready for the date to pump me full of words of encouragement. If I'm especially nervous, I ask the friend to walk with me toward the date location so I don't have TOO much time alone with my thoughts."

—MADELINE, 26, NEW YORK CITY

"Schedule a dinner or drinks date for a weeknight, on the later side—say, 8:30—and go to happy hour with friends or coworkers first. I'm not saying get sloshed, but ONE drink will take the edge off, and your friends will help distract you. Plus, you'll fool yourself into thinking, *This date can't be a big deal! I'm not taking it that seriously. I mean, I'm at a BAR first.*"

—MICHELLE, 29, NEW YORK CITY
(editor of HowAboutWe's *The Date Report*)

"I have a 'dresser,' a drink you have when you're getting dressed. Always white wine. Safe if you spill it."

—LAURA, 28, CHICAGO

"I pass the pre-date time in my apartment, trying on different dresses and sending photos of them to friends to vote on what I should wear. It makes me feel confident in my outfit."

—JOY, 30, PORTLAND, MAINE

LIQUID COURAGE

If you're going to drink before a date (ha! "if."), here are some safe bets:

DRY MARTINI

Clear, strong, whets the
appetite, and won't smell
on your breath.

SPARKLING WINE

Not too boozy, won't stain
your teeth, and you can finish a small glass quickly.

**ONE (JUST ONE!)
SHOT OF TEQUILA**

It's quick and gives
you energy.

GREEN TEA

Gives energy but won't make
you jittery, won't stain your teeth,
won't upset your stomach, and
won't go to your head.

OLD-FASHIONED

For when you're waiting for your
date at the bar. Classic, strong,
and can be sipped slowly (in
case you have a long wait).

ON THE DATE

YOU KNOW how people feed off of each other's energies? I know that sounds New Age-y, but it's true. You can tell when someone feels awkward, and then you feel awkward, vicariously. The point is, you can set the tone for your own date. If you act at ease and positive and friendly, your date will feel at ease and positive and friendly, and then you have the makings of a fun time.

And that should be your main goal on a first date—having fun with this person. Awkward moments and situations are bound to come up, but don't dwell or worry about them. Keep the conversation moving, ask questions, stay on light topics, and (this is important!) don't be afraid to let him know you're interested in him if you are! Eye contact, light touching, smiling—you know the drill.

47% of daters surveyed said drinking too much has ruined a first date.

Stick to one to three drinks, no more than that.

TEN THINGS YOU SHOULD KNOW
AT THE END OF A FIRST DATE

1. If he's gainfully employed

2. If he's cheap (as opposed to thrifty, which is fine)

3. If you have at least one thing in common

4. If you think he's funny

5. If he's smart

6. If he's insecure

7. If he has a kid

8. If he seems genuinely interested in you

9. If he's polite

10. If he talks about himself the whole time

AND FIVE THINGS YOU SHOULDN'T KNOW

1. How much money he makes

2. How awesome his ex is, and why they broke up

3. What he's like when he's really drunk

4. How many other dates he's been on lately

5. How hard he's working to overcome any issues/psychological problems/ setbacks

HOW TO ORDER

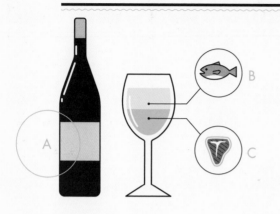

WINE

1. Stick to a label you can pronounce *(fig. A)*. If you can't pronounce it, skip the name and say the type you want.

2. Remember, white wine with fish *(fig. B)*, red wine with meat *(fig. C)*. Safe to stick with the region, so Italian wines with Italian food, etc.

3. Ask the waiter for a recommendation rather than ordering blindly, if you're not sure!

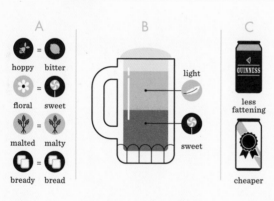

hoppy = bitter

floral = sweet

malted = malty

bready = bread

light

sweet

less fattening

cheaper

BEER

1. Learn some vocab *(fig. A)*. Hoppy = bitter. Floral = sweet. Malted = . . . malty. Bready = tastes like bread. Okay, you get it.

2. If you like a light taste, try a Belgian wheat beer *(fig. B)*. If you like sweet, ask for a brown beer *(fig. B)*. And if you hate beer, try Magic Hat #9 (readily available, and comes in flavors like apricot), cider (try Magner's), or lambic, which sort of tastes like an alcoholic strawberry soda.

3. Guinness is the beer with the fewest calories *(fig. C)*, and PBR tends to be the cheapest *(fig. C)*, if you're worried about either of those qualities.

x1

sweet

sour

bitter

COCKTAILS

1. Don't order something you don't like just to seem cool; it will show in your scrunched up face if it's too bitter or too strong for you.

2. Try to choose cocktails with one alcoholic ingredient *(fig. A)*, and stick to that alcohol all night.

3. If you're at a cocktail bar and don't know what to order, ask for a bartender's special. They'll ask your alcohol of choice and whether you like sweet, sour, or bitter *(fig. B)*, then whip something up based on your preferences.

ITALIAN FOOD

1. When in doubt, pronounce every syllable. Carpacio = *Car-pa-chee-oh*. Amatriciana = *Ah-ma-tree-chee-ah-nah*. *Ch-* actually makes a "k" sound, so bruschetta = *brews-KE-tah* (not *brew-SHET-ta*).

2. First course is pasta, second course is meat or fish *(fig. A)*. (Though in most Italian restaurants in the U.S., you certainly aren't expected to order both.)

3. There's no *x* in *espresso*, and a cappuccino is generally a morning beverage. Order coffee or an alcoholic "digestivo" with dessert or at the end of the meal *(fig. B)*.

first course   second course

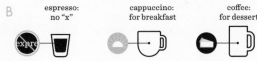

espresso: no "x"   cappuccino: for breakfast   coffee: for dessert

FRENCH FOOD

1. Au jus (*oh joos*) means something that is cooked/served in its own juices. (Gross in definition, but pretty tasty in practice.)

2. Steak frites (*steak freet*) = steak and fries. Vichyssoise = cold, leek and cream-based soup. Crepe Suzette = dessert.

3. *Grenouilles* and *escargot* mean frogs' legs *(fig. A)* and snails *(fig. B)*, respectively. Will you be kissing after this dinner date? Just curious.

A

grenouilles = frogs' legs

B

escargot = snails

SUSHI

1. Sushi is raw fish on rice; sashimi is just raw fish. If you want rolls, order maki. And if fish isn't your thing, look for gyoza (dumplings) or teriyaki.

2. Knowing how to properly use chopsticks is such a turn-on, it might be worth learning just so you can impress dates. A fork is perfectly fine, though. When sharing food, transfer food onto each other's plates by using the opposite end of the chopsticks that you put in your mouth.

3. When dipping your sushi into soy sauce, aim to have the fish, and not the rice, hit the sauce *(fig. A)*. The pink slivers are ginger, for cleansing your palate between plates. And if you've never had wasabi, the super-spicy green sauce *(fig. B)*, then a first date is *prooooobably* not the best time to test it out.

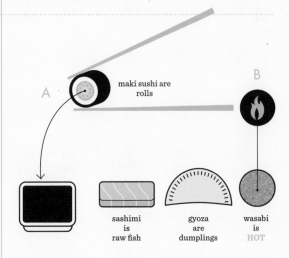

A   maki sushi are rolls   B

sashimi is raw fish   gyoza are dumplings   wasabi is HOT

WHO PAYS FOR THE DATE: THE NEW 50/50

HISTORICALLY, men have always paid for dates. Men had the jobs, men had the money; therefore it only made sense that men should offer to pay for dinner. Women simply weren't earning any money of their own. Then, in the second part of the twentieth century, "going dutch" began to get popular as women started earning income and questioning traditional courtship roles. If the man and the woman are equal in the relationship, it doesn't make sense for the man to always pay.

The problem, though, with splitting the bill "50/50" is that it assumes both people are able to spend the same amount of money, something which is increasingly rare. The disparity between pay rates of two young people in a city can sometimes be extreme. What's more, it's no longer safe to assume that it's the man who makes more money, despite that fact that men continue to feel the need or pressure to contribute.

The person who invited the other person out should probably offer to pay, with the understanding that if you continue to see each other, your date will foot the bill next time. This means that when planning a first date, you should choose something that you can afford to treat your date to. Don't choose an expensive activity if you can't pay for both.

If you got asked out, bring enough cash to cover your portion, just in case. Offer to pay once, and if he declines, don't insist. (THANK him!)

As the relationship progresses, who pays for the date should be determined by who makes the most money, but *both people* should be offering to pay with equal frequency.

In other words, both people in a relationship should be contributing regularly to the cost of courtship, but the actual financial investment should be proportionate to what each individual makes. And both should be *offering* to pay for things at an equal rate. If one person gets the movie tickets, the less financially flush person can get the popcorn. One person buys the fancy anniversary dinner, the other pays for the cab. The person who assumes the brunt of the financial burden, in terms of numbers, should of course be determined by paycheck and not by gender. Because gender isn't a determining factor, this system of pay parity works for hetero and gay couples alike.

In relationships where both parties make the same amount of money, switch off at equal rates—but *don't* split the check, which is unromantic at best and awkward at worst.

The important thing isn't who actually spends more, and at no point in the relationship should amounts be tallied and compared. The point is for both people in the relationship to be equally generous and giving in spirit, even if disparate in dollars and cents.

THE ECONOMICS OF DATING:
FOUR THINGS I'VE LEARNED ALONG THE WAY

HANNA ROSIN, *Author*, The End of Men

---

1. Your salary shouldn't determine your dating pool.

If you want economic independence and sexual independence, you're just going to have to accept that you might date some guys who make less money than you do and figure out if you're okay with that—if you're okay with paying two-thirds of the rent instead of half the rent.

2. It's okay to be the breadwinner and still expect chivalry.

I think that people can work through the financial issues, but they have a hard time working through the deep archetypal issues. Like man as protector: I think that's something that women kind of still want from men and men still want to be. You can make a lot less money than the women you're dating but still fulfill certain other notions of how a man should be and behave: that the man should make the first move, and a man should protect you, and a man should pick things up for you. I don't necessarily see these as contradictory.

3. Be aware of each other's financial limitations.

You don't have to work out your feelings about this right away, but if you are making more money and you guys are pretty serious, it's obnoxious to be constantly suggesting really expensive restaurants. Once you're in sort of the regular-going-out phase, you should talk about it.

4. Men don't want to be meal tickets.

I have plenty of guy friends who are really freaked out by the idea of their wives' *not* working and *not* contributing to the income. Sure, guys want to be providers. But that doesn't mean that they want, day to day, to be responsible for paying all the bills. Men these days are not really looking for a woman who expects to be completely taken care of.

HOW TO INITIATE THE END-OF-THE-NIGHT KISS

SOME GUYS ARE really good about leaning in and kissing you at just the right moment, so that you don't have to do any work apart from just . . . being kissable. These guys are great, because minimal effort means maximum enjoyment.

But other guys are shy and bumbling and give the impression that they'll never make a move unless you take matters into your own hands.

God, a woman has to do everything these days, doesn't she? Here's how to initiate a kiss.

1. First, you have to touch.

Don't run before you're ready to walk! Touch his waist, arm, hand, back, anything you can think of to establish physical contact.

2. Make eye contact with his lips.

If you two are talking, look at his mouth, which sends the subliminal message that you're thinking about kissing. It seems a bit obvious, but when it comes to making a first kiss happen, you *need* to be obvious. (I hasten to add: Don't stare *solely* at his mouth—break for a little eye contact now and then, and if after a while you still haven't gone in for a kiss, for God's sake *switch strategies*.)

3. Get close and lean in.

Going in for a kiss can be really scary, so for your sake, you want to make the transition time between not kissing and kissing as short as possible. To minimize the agonizing *Oh my Goddd* while your head travels to his, move in close. Know that once you get to a certain amount of closeness, even if you're just talking, it becomes pretty obvious that a kiss is going to happen. This is okay! You're both on the same page; otherwise he would move back and continue conversing at a normal distance.

4. Touch his face.

If you need one more beat before working up the nerve to kiss, touch his face or hair. It's intimate and sweet, and creates one more little bridge between "not kissing" and "kissing." Once you're ready (and seriously, don't take all night!), you can use your hand on his face or head to tilt his face toward yours or (gently! not insistently) pull him in.

If you've gotten this far without having the other person scoot as far away from you as possible, you can be pretty darn sure he wants to kiss you as much as you want to kiss him. So just close your eyes and move in.

AFTER THE DATE

A**FTER THE DATE** is over, you have an important decision to make: Do you want to go on *more* dates with this kid, or do you want to never go on another date with him again? If you had a nice time on your date, a follow-up text the next day is a must. The purpose of this text is simply to thank him for a fun afternoon/evening, so really don't stress out about it. If your date had a good time as well, he'll be stoked to hear from you, and if he *didn't*, well, whatever, you were just being polite.

"Hey, I had fun yesterday. Thanks again!"

If you want to allude to a "next time," you can try variations of . . .

"Next time, it's on me . . . " / "Rematch sometime soon . . . "

A third strategy is to simply text about something that you guys talked about on the date. But definitely don't overthink it: The point is to sound casual and natural, not scripted and overwritten.

If you're *not* into him, don't send a follow-up text. There's a chance that he won't contact you, which is the best-case scenario. But if he does ask you out again, you'll probably be tempted to just ignore the call or text. Zero awkward confrontation on your part, and he'll definitely get the point.

A more mature way to deal with it, though, is to send a nice text explaining that while you had a nice time with him (even if you didn't), it's not going to be going any further. ("I really enjoyed meeting you, but I don't think we're a good fit" is a gentle way to put it.) Believe me, he'll be upset for like, two seconds, but mostly grateful for your honesty.

AND IF HE NEVER CALLS YOU BACK...

Yeah, you liked him. Yeah, he was funny. Yeah, you "had a good feeling about this one." But for whatever reason, he wasn't feeling it, and if he wasn't feeling it, then *he isn't the right person for you!* You're holding out for the guy who can't *wait* to see you again, who has to give a friend his phone in order to resist calling you and asking you out again *right away*. Give yourself a day to feel bummed, then get yourself back out there.

75 Out-of-the-Box DATE IDEAS

There is nothing wrong with meeting someone for drinks, but if you've started to feel like all your dates begin and end on a bar stool, it might be time to branch out. Practically any activity can make a good date, but coming up with new and interesting date ideas can be tricky. If you need a little help, take a look at some of these possibilities—many of which we've borrowed from the daters on HowAboutWe.com. We're not suggesting you go mini-golfing or take a cooking class on every single date, but aim to make at least one date a month special and interesting. (And remember: Better dates = a better dating life.)

EAT

1. **Celebrate Taco Tuesday and sample the best taco trucks in the city.** $

2. Hit the farmer's market and get all the ingredients for the perfect picnic. $

3. Go to a bunch of chocolate shops and try all the free samples you can get your hands on. $

4. Go to a mall food court and revisit all your old favorites. $

5. Go to an Indian restaurant and ask them to give you the spiciest thing on the menu. $$

6. Go on a gelato or cupcake crawl and try a different flavor at each stop. $$

7. Take a cooking class together. $$$

8. Cook a meal inspired by one of your favorite books or movies. $$

9. Meet for a diner breakfast before work. $$

10. Book the chef's table at a restaurant and watch the chef work his magic in the kitchen. $$$

11. Plan a progressive dinner, with each of you picking a restaurant for a specific course, starting with appetizers and ending with dessert. $$$

12. Split a plate of meatballs at IKEA and peruse the knickknacks in the showroom. $

13. Go to a dim-sum restaurant and dare each other to taste everything, even if you don't always know what exactly you're eating. $$

EXPLORE

14. Meet in a used book store and pick out the strangest books you can find for each other to read. $

15. ## Bike out of the city, have lunch somewhere remote, and then head back. $ $

16. Find an old-fashioned carousel and try to grab the brass ring. $

17. Sneak a flask into the microfiche rooms at the public library, pick a random year, and read the old newspapers from back then. $

18. Go whale-watching (either on a boat or at the local aquarium). $ $

19. Pick a random number and let it dictate the number of stops you ride on the subway. Have lunch or dinner wherever you end up. $ $

20. Head to a graveyard and try to find the oldest headstone. $

21. Check out the dinosaur bones at the natural history museum. $ $

22. Wander around a botanical garden. $

23. Go to an art museum and choose a painting to buy for your house (in case you win the lottery). $ $

24. Rent a kayak, canoe, or paddleboat and spend an hour or two on whatever body of water is nearest. $ $

25. Play tourists in your own city and hit up all the major attractions. $ $

26. Go to a flea market and see who can go home with the weirdest purchase. $

PLAY

27. Take a surfing class and see if you can hang ten. $ $

28. Grab a bucket of sidewalk chalk and make a huge drawing. $

29. Take a yoga class together. $

30. ## Find the nearest roller coaster and see how many times you can bear to ride consecutively. $ $

31. Rent Rollerblades and spend the afternoon skating around like it's 1989. $

32. Go horseback riding at the local equestrian center. $ $ $

33. Head to the greens for a game of mini-golf. $ $

34. Test your aim at a local shooting range. $ $

35. Sneak into a hotel pool and pretend you're on vacation all day. $

36. Spend an evening at the nearest place with bumper cars or boats. $ $

37. Take a figure-drawing class together. $ $

38. Find a new running trail and meet for a morning run. $

39. Rent ice skates and see if you have any coordination on a rink. $ $

40. Go visit a string of psychics and see if any of their predictions match up. $ $

41. Take an improv class and try to make each other break character during a scene. $ $

42. Find a bingo hall and go try your luck. $ $

43. Play "bike and seek"—hide 'n' seek on bikes. $

44. Spend the afternoon on a bench sketching, and then exchange drawings when you're done. $

45. Go to the zoo on a rainy day. You'll have all the animals to yourselves! $ $

DRINK

46. Find a local brewery and go on a tour. $

47. Go to a Japanese tea house for an authentic tea service. $ $

48. Sample different wines at a local winery and see if you can actually distinguish any of the "notes." $ $

49. Get dressed up and meet for cocktails in a hotel bar. $ $

50. Go to a local dive bar and see who's better at pool (or darts, or drinking). $

51. ### Find a tiki bar and share a scorpion bowl. Stumble home afterward. $ $

52. Pick a random cocktail and do a taste test at three different bars to find the best one. $ $ $

53. Grab champagne and oysters after work one evening. $ $

54. Bring a Lite Brite to a bar and write each other messages. $

55. Have a coffee crawl—no Starbucks! $

56. Meet up for a late-night cup of hot chocolate (which may or may not be spiked). $

LISTEN/WATCH

57. Head to an open mic/ amateur night at a local bar and rate the talent (or lack thereof). $

58. Check out the new local talent at a comedy club. $

59. See if any old classic movies are playing at an independent movie theater. $

60. Bring two pairs of headphones and a laptop to a café, get snacks and drinks, and watch a movie on a rainy day. $

61. Pick out new music for each other to listen to at an indie music store. $

62. Get rush tickets to a concert at the local symphony or philharmonic. $$

63. Go to a minor league soccer game and try to get some spectator chants started. $$

64. Head to a drive-in theater and make up your own dialogue to the movie. $

65. Recreate the dates in *Pretty Woman/ Moonstruck* by going to an opera. $$$

66. Go see a movie, then sneak into another one. Double feature! $

67. Go to a museum, pick one room, and gaze at the tourists instead of the art. $

68. Borrow a projector, find a wall, and create a pop-up movie screening somewhere unexpected. $

VOLUNTEER

69. Walk the dogs at a local animal shelter. $

70. Help paint a local school or play-ground. $

71. Give blood together, and treat yourselves to blood-sugar–boosting treats afterward. $$

72. Wait for the next time it rains, and then go hand out umbrellas to people who don't have one. $$$

73. Serve a meal at a soup kitchen on a Saturday. $

74. Spend an afternoon doing a beach or park cleanup together. $

75. Volunteer at a local greenhouse or arbore-tum for the afternoon. $

Chapter 5

DATING

The
EARLY STAGES

I F THE WORLD were a fair place, then meeting someone you actually like would be the hardest part about dating. After all, you already went through all the work of flirting, arranging a meeting place, calibrating your expectations to "realistic yet hopeful," and actually going on the date. Now that you know that he likes you, it should be smooth sailing from here on out. *If* the world were fair.

Unfortunately, a good first date does not necessarily a fairy-tale ending make. The early stages of dating (between the second date and first three months or so) are full of tricky things to navigate. Learning how to have sex with each other, for instance. (Not how to *have sex*—hopefully you've figured that out or, like, read a book on that by now—but how to have sex *with each other* based on

individual quirks and preferences and desires.) Or figuring out how often you should see each other, and whether you're seeing each other exclusively, and how to bring that up. And what is your texting relationship going to be like, and can you friend each other on Facebook, and do you want to introduce him to your friends?

And what if, despite seeing each other consistently over time, you're still not sure how you *feel* about him, if you even like him that much? Or what if (even worse!) he tells you that he doesn't want to keep seeing you?

Even in the loveliest, easiest of circumstances, the initial stages of seeing someone are full of things to think about.

So before we get into all the intricacies (and trivialities) of dating, remember this:

Being able to state your feelings clearly and succinctly is a requirement of dating."

—Sarah, 26, Chicago

This is when you feel happy and sexy and giddy at the thought of meeting up after work. This is when you go shopping and buy a dress with the unspoken intention of wearing it on your next date with him, when you greet each other more warmly with the progression of each date, when he starts to recognize the characters in your life and you recognize the ones in his. When you make out in the back of the taxi and text without hesitation and build up a little collection of nicknames and inside jokes for two.

Maybe this will evolve into a long relationship, and maybe it won't, but the future trajectory of your relationship shouldn't be of too much concern now. Your major job is to simply figure out if you like this person enough to want another date . . . and another

one . . . and another after that. As long as the answer is yes, you'll deal with each development as it comes.

And if it doesn't work out, then you go on another first date and meet someone else, and repeat the process. That's dating. And each time around, you're gonna get a little bit better at it, a little bit more ready to deal if you should meet the love of your life tomorrow.

TEN CHARACTERISTICS OF AN AWESOME DATER

1. You view dates as an opportunity to meet someone new and have an interesting conversation.

2. You're open to the possibility of finding love. Every guy could end up being someone special, so you keep an open mind.

3. You date actively and schedule lots of dates with different guys, in order to keep from putting too much pressure on things early on.

4. But you still keep time in your schedule for friends/non-romantic recreation. Dating is important, but it's not your whole life.

5. You're in tune with your needs and wants, and you let those dictate your actions rather than "rules" or attempts to predict what the guy wants or expects.

6. You don't put pressure on yourself to find someone special or meet any sort of deadline.

7. You don't let yourself get discouraged after a bad date—it's all part of the process! You approach your dating life with both diligence and a light heart.

8. You say yes—to dates, to party invitations, to opportunities, and, when you feel like you need it, to quiet nights in with your feet up.

9. You're happy to date casually but won't settle when it comes to a serious relationship.

10. You don't overanalyze things, look for hidden meanings, or make excuses for the guys you date.

THE SECOND DATE

YOU WENT OUT, you liked each other, and you want to see each other again. Now what?

A second date is usually way easier and less stressful than the first. For one thing, you already know that you like each other, and that takes off a lot of the pressure. And given that you spent time with each other relatively recently, you presumably have things to talk about.

There is such a thing as a second-date slump, which is always a bummer, especially if the first date was awesome. When this happens, it's still probably worth giving him another chance, just to be sure that the good first date was the anomaly, and not the bad second.

The primary objective of early-stage dates (apart from having a good time together) is to start ascertaining whether or not you and he are looking for the same things. Do you want someone to date casually and see a few times a month? Or are you looking for a serious relationship? It will start to become clear by the second date which one he's interested in, and if your visions don't jibe, well, better to figure it out sooner rather than later.

And of course, during the first couple of dates, you're analyzing his character and personality as well as chemistry. If you *aren't* looking for a long-term relationship right now, then it's fine to date someone with whom you couldn't imagine yourself long-term. But if you want to find something serious, then it's important not to waste time dating someone who ultimately won't be right for you, so pay extra attention to compatibility.

A SMOOTH MOVE

If you're on a second date with someone you're really crazy about, you might consider busting out the move that TV personality Giuliana Rancic used to woo her now-husband, Bill Rancic. The couple had gone out to a restaurant, and toward the end of the meal, Giuliana excused herself to go to the restroom—and secretly walked to the front of the restaurant to pay the bill. The fact that she paid and pre-empted any debate or protestations on his part not only impressed him but also set a good precedent of equality within the relationship. Pretty foolproof way to impress!

The Most Popular DATES IN AMERICA

Since we first launched HowAboutWe, we've had over 1 million dates posted from around the country. Here are some of the most popular date ideas, city by city.

SEATTLE
How about we... catch the late-night Pink Floyd laser show at the Pacific Science Center.

PORTLAND
How about we... meet at Powell's City of Books, each find one of our favorite books, and discuss over coffee.

DENVER
How about we... get lost in the giant cornfield maze at Denver Botanic Gardens.

LAS VEGAS
How about we... go on a tour of the factory and botanical cactus garden at Ethel M Chocolate Factory.

KANSAS CITY
How about we... hit up an amusement park.

SAN FRANCISCO
How about we... sample the different flavors of home-made coffee at Philz Coffee shop.

AUSTIN
How about we... head to Peter Pan for a friendly round of BYOB mini-golf, then talk strategy over burgers at Hopdaddy's.

LOS ANGELES
How about we... hike through Griffith Park to the observatory and see a show at the planetarium.

SAN DIEGO
How about we... grab drinks at the Prado before catching a play at the Old Globe.

PHOENIX
How about we... try the bison burgers and pomegranate mojitos at True Food Kitchen.

SAN ANTONIO
How about we... pair the rocket tots with two of the 100+ beers on offer at the Flying Saucer.

MINNEAPOLIS
How about we... watch the dogs play over a picnic and Frisbee at Minnehaha Park.

CHICAGO
How about we... volunteer at the Shedd. Maybe we'll get to swim with the dolphins!

CLEVELAND
How about we... try the loaded hot dogs and homemade ice cream at Ohio City Ice Cream Company.

NEW YORK CITY
How about we... go bowling and have some amazing fried chicken at Brooklyn Bowl.

PITTSBURGH
How about we... ride some of the scariest rides at Kennywood, then reward our bravery with funnel cake.

ST. LOUIS
How about we... take a motorcycle ride along the river road and picnic in Grafton.

BOSTON
How about we... check out the latest exhibits at the ICA and follow with drinks at the Whiskey Priest.

DETROIT
How about we... support the local stand-up acts at Mark Ridley's Comedy Castle.

PHILADELPHIA
How about we... have lunch at the World Café, then walk over to the Penn Museum to spend the afternoon with the mummies.

DALLAS
How about we... discuss our favorite finger food over an indoor cheese picnic at Scardello Artisan Cheese.

WASHINGTON, D.C.
How about we... grab a beer at the Bullpen and then catch a Nats game.

ATLANTA
How about we... pack a brunch picnic and fly kites at Piedmont Park.

ORLANDO
How about we... ride the swan boats at Lake Eola followed by a picnic in the park.

HOUSTON
How about we... sample craft beers during a tour of the Saint Arnold Brewing Company.

TAMPA
How about we... enjoy an authentic Spanish dinner and live flamenco-dance show at the Columbia Restaurant

MIAMI
How about we... explore the galleries at Wynwood Art Walk while sampling the croquetas from Cuban Cube.

GUYS TO WATCH OUT FOR...

NOT TO PIGEONHOLE men into unfair stereotypes, but there are certain types of guys that are simply difficult and/or unpleasant to date. (You probably have a girlfriend who dates these guys over and over again . . . .)

Be on the lookout early on, *especially* if you're looking for a serious relationship. A guy who exhibits any of the following tendencies might honestly be more trouble than he's worth.

❋ The Guy Who Needs to Be Admired

It's not enough for you to tell him he's smart and funny and attractive. He needs to feel it and hear it from other people, too, and he's willing to work for it by constantly flirting with other people via email, at parties, in line at the grocery store, among the wait staff of restaurants . . . everywhere. Even though he won't straight-out cheat, you'll never feel like you're enough for this guy, because, well, you aren't.

❋ The Guy Who Has Friends You Never Meet

He's always emailing, texting, or running off to see "friends," but you're never invited to come along. It's not that you suspect he's cheating on you, but a guy who compartmentalizes his life like this is clearly not ready to share it with anyone else. Or he's ashamed of you, or he's ashamed of *them*. Either way, *no bueno*.

❋ The Guy Who Hates His Job

Hating your job—where you spend the majority of your time—is a destructive mind-set that can poison a relationship. It's one thing to be mildly dissatisfied with work life *while at work*, but the guy who is absolutely miserable at his job will spend a good amount of his free time being absolutely miserable about it as well, and that's not good.

You *don't* want to date a guy who gets stuck in an unhappy situation and doesn't do anything about it. Is this what he's going to be like if there are relationship problems down the line?

❋ The Guy Who's Obsessed with His Mother

He loves her, defers to her, consults her about everything, and you will never live up to her.

Or he hates her, constantly complains about her, and expects you to be the complete opposite of her.

Simply put: There isn't enough room in a relationship for you, him, and the giant Shadow of His Mother.

❋ The Guy Who Wants to Rescue You

For some reason, he always seems to date people who are complete basket cases, because he likes to play the hero. He gets off on coming in and acting as a stabilizing force, rescuing women from their situations or themselves, advising, helping, tranquilizing. The more messed-up a woman is, the more attracted he feels: He *needs* to feel needed. But the second her life starts to get in order, he loses interest, because without her issues to take the focus away from him, he's left with his own problems and insecurities to deal with. And *that* he absolutely cannot do.

❋ The Guy Who Can't Believe You Picked Him

At first, it's flattering and endearing that this guy seems to think he's so out of your league. He just can't believe that you would ever be attracted to a guy like him, such a loser. In fact, he goes on and on about this, for so long that eventually you start to believe him. His constant need for validation and reassurance from you makes you feel more like his guardian than his girlfriend.

THE DATING-AGE-RANGE FORMULA

To find out what the youngest age you should date is, take your current age, divide it by 2, and add 7.*

$$\text{CURRENT AGE} \div 2 + 7 = \text{YOUNGEST AGE}$$

To find out what the oldest age you should date is, take your current age, subtract 7, and multiply it by 2.*

$$\text{CURRENT AGE} - 7 \times 2 = \text{OLDEST AGE}$$

* Honestly, there's no such thing as being "too old" or "too young" for someone if you're compatible, but this old-school "formula" is fun to play around with.

TIPS FOR DATING IN THE WORKPLACE

WHEN I POLLED my friends on Facebook and Twitter for advice on dating a co-worker, the overwhelming majority of the responses were simply, *"Don't."* It seems like everyone has a cautionary tale of a relationship in a workplace that went terribly, terribly wrong. Dating a co-worker or boss or colleague can lead to unbearable awkwardness, a tarnished professional reputation, and even job loss.

Like that's going to stop anybody from doing it.

For as long as there have been workplaces, there have been people surreptitiously hooking up at them.

So if you're gonna do it (and chances are, you're gonna do it), here are some tips on getting through with minimal heartache/trips to HR.

❋ Don't treat work as extended quality time.

One of the great injustices of society is that most of us are expected to show up someplace five days a week and perform a task in exchange for money. It sucks, but until we all leave to form a utopian society on Mars, that's the way it's going to be. If you guys are at work, you're supposed to be *working*.

It's important to keep your at-work relationship as professional as possible: Unless you're at lunch or in a group setting, try to limit the non-work-related small talk to after-hours.

❋ Send surreptitious flirty text messages to each other.

You're crazy about each other but aren't allowed to openly express it when you're at work together. Clearly, this is a recipe for some insane sexual tension. But communicating via the company email system is dicey, and any email you open on your computer screen can be too easily read by a co-worker. Send each other text messages instead— not too often, but enough to keep things interesting. (But don't send angry texts— save the serious for after work.)

❋ Don't go to lunch together every day.

Ah, lunch! The recess of the adult world. Though it's tempting to treat every lunch hour like a midday date with the co-worker you're sleeping with, it's a good idea to either set a schedule or limit your lunches together to one day a week. You really don't want to become "that couple," to the exclusion of your other co-workers, and you also don't want to spend *too* much time together (and risk burnout!).

❄ If one of you manages the other, just don't date, period.

Don't date or sleep with your boss or subordinate. It puts both of you in an awkward (and fireable!) position, and things like "sexual harassment" get too easy to claim. If you *really* think this might be the love of your life, consider leaving your job before you start a relationship. If it's just a fling you're after, don't do it.

❄ Be wary of keeping it "secret."

You might *think* you're keeping your relationship completely secret, but there's no real way to ensure this. Keep this in mind if having an affair in your office is a fireable offense.

❄ Once it's a relationship, go public (to the necessary parties) ASAP.

If you and a co-worker actually start dating and plan on being a couple for a while, stop keeping it a secret. Tell your bosses/HR representatives/whoever needs to know, and assure them that you'll continue to keep your work life as professional as possible. From then on, keep things as open, yet unsalacious, as possible.

❄ Have a breakup contingency plan.

The biggest objection people seem to have to dating a co-worker is the inevitable awkwardness of going to work post-breakup. As weird as it may seem, it's super-helpful to discuss what you'll do if and when things don't work out. One couple I know agreed up front to avoid the "Fadeout" method of breaking up (see page 163), since they had to see each other every day at work. They agreed that the second either one wasn't feeling it anymore, they'd be up front about it and the relationship would end, full stop: no unnecessary drama.

❄ Make out in the elevator.

Secretly making out in the elevator at work and then stopping the second you get to your floor is a fantasy everyone has, and you have the opportunity to make it happen. Take advantage, on behalf of the rest of us.

SIGNS HE'S DEFINITELY INTO YOU

☐ **1.** He remembers things about you and asks you questions about your job/life/ hobbies.

☐ **2.** He finds random excuses to email or text you. ("Thought you might like this generic Internet meme!"; "That movie starring that actor that we briefly talked about on our last date is on! Just thought you should know!")

☐ **3.** He compliments you. Not in an offhanded way that you have to later repeat to your girlfriends in order to actually ascertain that it was, in fact, a compliment, but in a direct, no-bones-about-it way.

☐ **4.** He goes out of his way to be nice to your friends (and maybe gets a little nervous before meeting them).

☐ **5.** He calls when he says he'll call; he shows up when he says he'll show up. He goes out of his way to see/listen to/read anything you've mentioned you've liked, and he'll tell you about it.

☐ **6.** When you see him, he says things like, "Oh, I was thinking of you the other day when ____." Because he *thinks about you*, you see.

☐ **7.** He makes up a nickname for you.

☐ **8.** He talks to his friends about you.

☐ **9.** He always makes plans for the next time you'll see each other. He doesn't leave things open-ended.

...AND SIGNS *YOU'RE* REALLY INTO *HIM*

☐ **1.** You find yourself casually clicking over to his or her Facebook page or Twitter account . . . six times a day.

☐ **2.** You talk to everyone about him. Like that co-worker you randomly ran an errand with. Like your grandma's sister at a family reunion. Like the ONE person who happens to be on Gchat when you get a cryptic text that you immediately need help decoding.

☐ **3.** You make plans with any mutual acquaintances you may have, in the hope that maybe, just maybe, he will come up in casual conversation. And if he doesn't, you bring him up.

☐ **4.** You can't help but thoroughly research anyone who tweets at him, writes on his wall, or gets tagged in a photo with him.

☐ **5.** You wouldn't say you have unrealistic expectations about this relationship, but when pressed, you admit you've *thought* about where you'll retire, and what activities you'll do with your eventual grandchildren.

☐ **6.** You absolutely refuse to make any plans for the weekend UNTIL you've made plans with him.

☐ **7.** It's so weird, but you can relate almost any conversation to one you were *just* having with him!

☐ **8.** Between dates, you find yourself renting movies he mentioned, reading his favorite book, idly Wikipedia-ing any anecdote he mentioned, and looking up flights to where he said he'd most like to go on vacation.

YOUR PLACE
AND HIS

WHEN YOU'RE seeing someone regularly, you're presumably going to see where he lives. This can actually be sort of a game changer. It's one thing to hang out with a person in a public space, but seeing what his place is like really contextualizes things. (Remember that episode of *Friends* where Ross is dating a beautiful blonde who turns out to have a disgustingly messy apartment? It was called "The Dirty Girl," and it traumatized me to the point where I now refuse to invite anyone over unless I've deep-cleaned my room beforehand.)

Talking about each other's favorite books and movies at a restaurant is different from seeing what is actually on each other's shelves. Seeing someone's neatly organized closet can be endearing, their mess of clothes and books can be charming, their choice of art on the walls impressive (or worrying, or whatever). The point is, someone's living space really paints a clear picture of what he's like.

And it's also a big deal for you to be *in* his space, or he in yours. You aren't in neutral territory anymore, so it might take time for you to be completely comfortable in each other's space. Which is fine—you'll get there eventually.

There's no reason to worry too much about inviting someone over for the first time. Your space is an extension of your personality, and you know he already likes that. The same is true for his place. You like the guy, so try not to judge his books/posters/action-hero collection *too* harshly, if you are so inclined.

HOW TO JUDGE A GUY BY HIS COVER

LAUREN LETO, *Author,* Judging a Book by Its Lover

WHEN YOU'RE meeting someone new, snap judgments are sometimes necessary. You're one person up against a sea of hundreds of thousands of eligible people, and there's no time to get to know everyone's life story. Reading selections can be an obvious giveaway of bad and good life habits, as the nuances in these choices are often indicative of much larger issues. The following is my attempt to categorize the most egregious and appealing types of book behavior.

❋ **Refuses to ditch his print books, screeches about the rise of e-books**

Do you want to be stuck with the pedantic twit who just can't let things go for the rest of your life? This man or woman will be the loudest member of the PTA someday, the type who sends dishes back in a restaurant if they're not cooked properly, the person who reads the front page of newspapers and thinks he understands it all.

❋ **Immediately embraces e-books, throws out printed books, brags about the extra space in his apartment**

This person gets over things way too quickly. There's no sentimentality, no nostalgia. Don't be surprised if he manages to just as quickly leave you and then wonders why you need closure.

❋ **Reads *Infinite Jest* on subway**

Possibly a psychopath.

❋ **Publicly admits *50 Shades of Grey* is his favorite book**

That book is for alone time, and alone time only. Maybe he's trying to weed out the meek from the misogynistic kinks, in which case, if you're down, go for it. If not, stay far away.

❋ **Reads a reasonably sized book that you've also enjoyed while sitting at a bar**

Go after this guy. Make conversation.

❋ **Reads *The Republic of Plato* at a bar**

Stay away. Unless you're in a college town, in which case he might just be trying to get his homework done while drinking.

❋ **Favorite author is P. G. Wodehouse**

Pretentious, arrogant. Pass, unless you secretly wish your name were Bitsy.

❋ **Favorite author is Joyce Carol Oates**

Delicate, prone to fainting fits. Pass, unless you enjoy leading someone by the arm.

❋ **Doesn't read**

Decide for yourself. Take it or leave it. Make sure he has some sort of art in his life, though; it makes people better.

The Pros and Cons of
YOUR PLACE

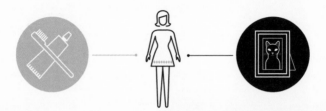

PROS	CONS
1. Home-court advantage! It's way easier to relax when you know your way around, know where everything is, know your roommates, etc.	1. You can't casually slip out of your own house before he wakes up.
2. You know for sure when the sheets were last washed.	2. The added pressure (and possible embarrassment) of having him see your things, your photographs, your mess.
3. You have your contact solution, your birth control, your toothbrush.	3. Sometimes it's less awkward to run into strangers the morning after than it is to run into your own roommates.
4. You don't have to ask for a glass of water.	4. That feeling, even when you like someone, of just wanting him to GET OUT the next morning.
5. No walk of shame.	5. Your sheets will smell like him the next day. When you regret inviting someone over, that's a really bad thing.
6. Your sheets will smell like him the next day. When you really, really like a guy, that's actually a good thing.	6. Your room is sacred. To invite a guy over and taint the room with the memory of someone else might be a big risk.
7. You can kick him out whenever you want!	

The Pros and Cons of
HIS PLACE

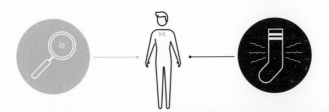

PROS	CONS
1. Oh my God, are you kidding? You get to see where he *lives*! This is going to tell you so much. I hope you bring a camera, a notepad, and a black light.	1. It can take a long time to get comfortable enough to actually *sleep* at someone else's place, in someone else's bed.
2. He's gonna be the one who's a little nervous, running in before you to clean up the mess, digging around for an extra towel, getting you a glass of water, etc. It's nice not having to play host!	2. His place might be a total shithole, and you'll judge him for it.
3. His place might be nicer—like, way nicer—than yours. Not that you should date a guy for his amenities, but . . .	3. Just because you can leave whenever you want to doesn't mean it's easy. You have to know where you are well enough to find your way home/direct a taxi.
4. It might actually be easier for you to sort of *let go* when you're outside of your own environment, what with its constant stressors and reminders of work to do, dishes to wash, bills to pay.	4. You don't have any of your *stuff* there.
5. You can leave whenever you want to.	5. Going home the next morning. It's not that you're ashamed; it's that you're tired and really want a shower.

GETTING YOUR APARTMENT READY FOR A GUY

B ECAUSE YOUR home is your home and not, say, a bordello, you really don't need to worry about making it "man-friendly" for potential dates, boyfriends, or one-night stands. You live there; he doesn't. Don't overhaul your apartment for a guy. (Obviously.)

That said, there's nothing wrong with making your apartment "date-ready," if by "date-ready" you mean a place where a romantic partner can feel relatively comfortable and where you can engage in adult activities without it feeling incongruous with the decor. (For instance, would you have sex with a guy who had Spiderman sheets? Maybe when drunk, and then you'd probably haul him out to Bed, Bath & Beyond the second things started to take a turn for the serious.)

In order to prime your room for overnight visitors of the sexual variety, start by getting rid of any lingering pictures of your ex-boyfriend. Photographs of Nana or your adorable baby nephew are okay in moderation, but it's best to keep those as far from the bed as possible. (Do you want to make accidental eye contact with a photograph of your grandmother while having sex? Do you want your date to?!)

Any fetishistic items should be put away, unless your date already knows about them. Make sure to have a fresh set of sheets on the bed. The nicer the sheets, the more inviting the bed (I'm talking sex *and* sleep here). Do you like the lights on or off while you're having sex? If you like them on, make sure to invest in some sort of lamp or dimmer so that the glaring overhead isn't your only option. If you prefer lights off, a thick lampshade keeps you from blindly fumbling around in the pitch black. Too many lit candles can be a bit much, but one or two can do a lot for atmosphere. If you live with roommates, a wall hanging or a tapestry will help soundproof the room a bit, as will a nice rug.

EMERGENCY SPEED-CLEANING

You've got six minutes. Here's your plan:

• Pick up all your dirty clothes from the floor and put them . . . in the hamper? In the closet? Under the bed? Whatever! Get rid of them.
• Put all the dirty dishes in the sink. Do not invite him into the kitchen.

• Make the bed! A room looks ten times cleaner when the bed is made. Who cares if you'll undo it in five minutes?
• Turn off all the lights in any room you won't be hanging out in, and lead him immediately to the bedroom.
• Light some candles. Apologize for the mess.

USEFUL SKILLS FOR STAYING OVER

In case you wind up at his house, these skills might come in handy:

❄ How to Brush Your Teeth Without a Toothbrush

Wet a paper towel and dab it with toothpaste. With your finger, work the paper towel across your top and bottom teeth with a gentle kneading motion. Rinse.

❄ How to Fall Asleep Anywhere

If you're not tired, you're not going to fall asleep. So if you're wide awake, maybe consider going home rather than forcing yourself to spend the night, which could turn into lying awake for hours in the dark. If it's too late to go home and the guy has already fallen asleep, see if you can stealthily grab your iPod and listen to some relaxing tunes or an especially soporific podcast. Don't freak out about being awake. Take deep breaths, chill out, and let your mind wander.

❄ How to Get Ready with No Makeup

Try and drink a glass of water before you go to sleep, and again when you wake up. Dehydration is part of what makes your skin look, well, let's say not the best after a night of drinking, so the more you hydrate, the better your skin will look. Now, get into the bathroom and raid his medicine cabinet for Vaseline or a Q-tip or something. If you don't have either, take some toilet paper, roll it up, and dab a tiny bit of soap on the tip. (If he doesn't have soap in the bathroom, you should just leave and never come back.) Carefully wipe the makeup from under your eyes and over your eyelids, but try to leave the mascara on, as well as a *tiiiiny* bit of eyeliner (or smudged makeup, whatever) around your eyelids. Gently slap your cheeks a bit to give yourself a little color, maybe hop around a bit to get your circulation going. (Make sure he doesn't walk in on you while you're doing this!) Dab some Vaseline on your lips, and you're good to go!

56% of women surveyed
prefer going to their own place at the end of a night.

SOCIAL MEDIA

and

TECHNOLOGY

EVEN THOUGH we're an online-dating site, we at HowAboutWe strongly believe that chemistry happens *offline*. You can't really build a relationship on a computer, and tweeting, texting, and messaging don't matter half as much as your in-person dynamic.

That said, social media nowadays bleeds into all aspects of life, including dating. We're no longer waiting by the phone for someone to call, because our phones are constantly in our hand. We text at movies, we check Facebook at parties, we chat with friends all day at work. Not only can we constantly interact with the people we're dating, but we often do it on public forums so everyone can see what we say to each other.

It's not all bad, of course. Sometimes a message or a tweet in the middle of the day can do wonders to stoke the fire of a relationship. Being able to look someone up before a blind date is useful. And a good texting session is one of the best things to happen to romance since the sonnet.

But it's easy to get the online relationship confused with the offline one. It's easy to misinterpret what someone says in 140 characters. It's easy to feel frustrated and ignored when someone *isn't* communicating 24/7 when you know he has the technological capability to do so.

So yeah, this stuff is important. But tread carefully. And when things start to get too confusing, close the browser window, turn off your phone, and wait to see each other in person.

TEXTING

THERE'S AN old-fashioned belief that when it comes to dating, a phone call is better, more mature, than a text message. This is true in certain situations—like if you're calling to talk about something serious or have to cancel a date.

At other times, texting can be a godsend for a dater. It lets you plan out what you're going to say, revise it, and get it approved by friends. If you're trying to play it cool, it's easier to do so via text. A text, at times, lets you say what you're too shy to say in person. ("You're cute," "I really like you," etc.)

If you're planning on seeing someone Wednesday, texting back and forth a bit on Monday can be a great mode of sustained flirtation. And if you're seeing someone *that*

night, think of the pre-date text message as sort of extended foreplay.

And a text says so much about the person you're dating. A perfect text message requires wit, brevity, and flirtation. A good texter is smart, sharp, and good with words. Additionally, someone who uses unnecessary text abbreviations or, God help him, too many emoticons can be flagged as potentially unworthy.

But the best thing about a text message is that it's forever. You can read that thing again and again, you can show your friends, you can memorize it, you can take out your phone and look at it throughout the day. In an era in which people don't send love letters anymore, a text is honestly the next best thing.

WHEN TO TEXT VS. WHEN TO CALL

- You're running five minutes late. **Text.**
- You're running an hour late. **Call. Apologetically.**
- You've gone on one date and you want to call to chat. **Don't.**
- It's his birthday. **Call.**
- You're on your lunch break, but he might not be. **Text.**
- He's having a shitty day at work. **Text.**

- You're having a shitty day at work. **Text. He should call later.**
- He got fired. **Call.**
- You're turned on and thinking about last night. **Text, unless you know he's alone.**
- It's time to plan the next date. **Call.**
- You're seeing if he's around on a weekend night. **Text.**

WHEN TECHNOLOGY ISN'T YOUR FRIEND

Technology has done a lot of great things for our dating lives. If nothing else, we're grateful that waiting for a guy to call doesn't mean physically waiting at home by the phone, like it did thirty years ago. So, yes, hurrah for cell phones and Facebook and email. That said, the opportunities for awkwardness and frustrations via technology abound.

"Once I liked everything and commented on his Facebook page, and if you do that, he's going to get scared out of his mind."
—BETH, 25, BOSTON

"If you keep calling and he keeps texting you back one-word answers, he's not really interested."
—MARISSA, 26, LOS ANGELES

On whom to friend on Facebook:
"Siblings OK, parents no, not unless you're married."
—MEGAN, 27, PITTSBURGH

"Gchat is great until you realize you're spending hours at a time talking to someone you haven't seen in real life in weeks. Then suddenly it starts to feel like a problem."
—MEGHAN, 29, TAMPA

"I have accidentally hit 'send' on unfinished emails to guys way more times than I care to remember! Now, if I'm writing to a guy I like, I don't put his e-mail address in until I am totally and completely finished perfecting the note."
—ALISON, 35, CHARLOTTE

"Never (ever) look at his Facebook page on a touch-screen phone. You will inevitably 'like' something by accident. If it's a vacation photo, that's one thing . . . but if it's a photo of him and his ex, well, that gets awkward."
—MARY KATE, 32, BROOKLYN

"I've kind of had my fill of Facebook stalking. Seeing all my ex-boyfriends looking super-happy with their hot new girlfriends just isn't that awesome."
—CARRIE, 24, DETROIT

TWITTER

T WITTER IS more than just a platform for self-promotion and witty commentary: It's a great way to interact and engage with someone you may not know all that well. And because Twitter is a medium expressly created for witty repartee, in the early stages of dating, you may feel more comfortable replying to a tweet than you would, for instance, writing on his Facebook wall. (At this point in the game, a tweet is just lower stakes, whereas a Facebook post is practically a public declaration of love.)

So how do you use Twitter to convey interest? Easy.

1. Direct Message

Taking it to Direct Message is, like, the Twitter equivalent of third base. You two are in a *private conversation* now—this is no offhand Twitter reply. Feel free to ramp up the flirtatious edge to what you say.

2. Follow Friday

Follow Friday is maybe the stupidest Internet convention ever (second only to Gratuitous Picture of Yourself Wednesday, on Tumblr), but even the most curmudgeonly Twitter follower can't help but be flattered to see himself on someone else's list. (Ex: #FF to @scienceguy, who manages to make even microbes sound quippy.) Yeah, it's silly, but when it comes to flirting, a little flattery never hurt anyone.

3. Retweet/Reply

Twitter is an interactive medium: Take advantage and retweet/reply to your crush's (no doubt brilliant) musings. At minimum, he'll see your little face pop up on his feed and, well, know you exist. At best, he'll start replying/retweeting you back.

Of course, ardent retweeting does not a relationship make. And whatever you do, don't retweet *everything,* for fear of coming off as a little . . . maniacal.

4. "Favorite" a Tweet

"Favoriting" a tweet is only slightly more evolved than, say, a Facebook poke. It basically means "I saw/appreciated what you just wrote but don't really have anything to say in response." A little passive, yes, but again a nice way to let someone know you're actively reading him/think he's funny. (If you favor multiple tweets in a row, it shows that you're *really* paying attention to his presence on Twitter.)

FACEBOOK

———

I MET A GUY recently who told me he wasn't on Facebook. I was horrified. How was I going to look at all his pictures and ascertain that he was single and give him an easy way to communicate with me?! Like it or not, Facebook has become instrumental in the dating world, an important way of communicating and learning about each other. This is good and bad. On the good side, you can learn a lot about a guy by closely monitoring his Facebook page. On the bad side, you can drive yourself crazy closely monitoring his Facebook page. And remember, there's also the chance that he's closely monitoring you.

Should you give up Facebook altogether for the sake of your sanity and love life? Probably. But until that day comes, here are some basic Facebook dating tips.

FRIENDING SOMEONE YOU'RE SEEING

When you become Facebook friends with someone, you're often giving him full access to the last however-many years of your life: what you looked like, whom you hung out with, maybe even whom you've dated. It's a lot of information, so friend judiciously, and before hitting "confirm," do a sweep of your profile.

Click on your most recent photos, and make sure you're okay with them. (Take a moment to untag the annoying and generic "Happy Thanksgiving!" post that your Aunt Sylvia always tags you in, etc.) Are there pictures of you tagged with someone who is clearly an ex-boyfriend? It's no secret that you've had previous relationships, but it can be intimidating for someone you just started dating to be able to look at the romantic-vacation photos you took with your ex last spring. Of course, you can always change the settings so he can't *see* your pictures, but if that's too drastic, just edit them.

Once you're officially Facebook friends, you can interact with him on the medium as much or as little as you wish, but make sure to read his signals, too. (Don't "like" every single thing he says, etc.) And remember, Facebook is public. Not everyone is comfortable with his extended social network reading into who is liking and commenting on his wall. If that's the case—for either of you!—then keep the Facebooking light.

If you're seeing other people, don't go overboard with the Facebook flirting. It's not hard for people to insinuate things.

HOW TO BREAK UP ON FACEBOOK

Say you were dating someone, but now you aren't anymore. How to deal with the delicate matter of your Facebook relationship? Easy:

If you instigated the breakup, give your ex a few days to take down the "In a Relationship" status first himself. It's a small, surprisingly empowering gesture that can help him feel a little less dumped. But if, after a few days, he still hasn't done it, go ahead and pull the trigger yourself—you don't want to lead him on or give him any reason to believe you're having second thoughts.

But if *you* were the one who got dumped, rip that Band-Aid off! Better you do it than your ex!

DATERS

YES 66%

NO 34%

About ⅔ of daters surveyed by HowAboutWe.com

admit to regularly stalking their crushes on Facebook.

GCHAT

GCHAT IS perfect for wasting away the workday, talking to your friends about nothing, but it presents all sorts of hazards for new relationships: Gchat fights, Gchat veiled comments that need immediate analysis, Gchat-related fatigue.

The problem with Gchat is that while an email chain will usually have a conclusive end ("Great, see you then!"; "Ha, hilarious, thanks for sending!"; "Reservation under 'Smith'"), a Gchat box stays open long after you've finished saying what you need to say. And when there's an empty box on your screen all day, most people are compelled by a completely human urge to *fill* it.

After all, it's hard to end a Gchat conversation without signing off, and most people, at work anyway, won't sign off until the end of the day. So how do you say, "Okay, great, I'm done talking to you now, even though I'm still sitting here," to someone you're dating? It's very difficult. The other option is the fadeout, but most people (girls? people?) panic at the thought of letting a conversation just peter out, as if it's an indication of boredom or lack of interest.

So the Gchat keeps going, and going, and going, peppered with mundane observations and halfhearted "lol"s. Even the best Gchats, the ones that are flirty and witty and exciting, lose their charm at some point. It's hard to sustain!

And of course, it's nearly impossible to really gauge the other person's reaction. At the beginning of a relationship, couples don't know each other well enough to interpret tone from a few lines of possibly misleading text: Jocular? Sarcastic? Offended? Or worse, bored? It is way too early in the relationship to analyze your date based on 12-point Helvetica.

And then, four hours later, you're finally on a *date* with the person, except you have nothing to say, because you spent the entire day catching up in your chat box.

Again, too early for that. Keep that magic alive. Stay off of Gchat.

PUTTING A GOOGLE ALERT ON SOMEONE YOU'RE DATING

> "I've been dating this guy for a month and a half. We were on a date the other night, and I told him excitedly about this website that I had just gotten mentioned on, and he said, 'Oh, I know, I saw it on your Google Alert.' He set up a Google Alert on me. After a month and a half. Is this weird?"
>
> —EMILY, 27, BROOKLYN

Huh . . .

Having a Google Alert on yourself makes sense. Having a Google Alert set up for someone you're *dating* is a different matter entirely.

On the one hand, it's flattering that he cared enough to want to be alerted of any professional developments the moment they happened.

On the other hand . . . too much too soon? Kind of . . . overzealous? I publicly pride myself on being a grade-A stalker, but I can't imagine actually signing up for a Google Alert on someone I'm dating: It would feel much too controlling/creepy. Besides, it totally takes the fun out of sharing exciting news with your partner. Does he *really* need to be kept abreast of every time you tweet, blog, or make an appearance on the Internet? Save something to talk about for the actual date!

Weird. A little stalkerish. Definitely weird.

69%

69% of daters surveyed by HowAboutWe.com think that setting up a Google Alert on someone you're dating is weird.

IF THINGS
DON'T WORK OUT

THINGS DON'T always work out. Even things that looked pretty promising. It sucks, because all breakups suck. Even the ones that were a long time coming, even the ones that you never expected to really last in the first place. The thing you've got to remember is that breakups are good for you in the long run. Really! Ending a relationship that isn't working just makes way for a relationship that does. Not that this is much comfort in the moment, when all you want to do (understandably!) is wallow in your misery.

So do yourself a favor and wallow away. Talk to your friends about it ad nauseam. Watch all the sad movies you can find. Listen to power ballads at full blast and dance around your room and start to feel better and then feel worse all over again. Whatever you need to get through it.

But the breakup period's got to be finite. Let yourself mourn to your heart's content for a period of time, and then stop. Pick yourself up by the bootstraps. You might not feel completely ready to get back out there. You might still be a little sad. That's natural! But breakups *stop* being healthy and start being harmful when you just can't seem to let go. (You *know* when you do this: It's when you sense your friends are losing patience with you, when you keep finding reasons to contact him, when your breakup starts coloring all other aspects of your life.)

Part of being a good dater is the ability to recover from heartbreak and move on to the next person—the person who *wants* to be with you. Don't waste too much time crying over the wrong one.

THE IN-PERSON BREAKUP TALK

THERE'S THIS pervasive idea that a face-to-face conversation is the most mature way to handle a breakup. It's also sort of the suckiest. It sucks for you, obviously, because it's scary and awkward and nerve-wracking to have to end it with someone and see his reaction. But it sucks for him, too. In a casual relationship, an in-person breakup can seem especially cruel, like, "You dragged me all the way out to this diner just to *break up with me?* Is this a *breakup* breakfast??" If you haven't been dating that long, you might as well give the person the option of just hanging up on you, or deleting your email and promptly forgetting you exist. I mean, it's the humane thing to do.

But if you've been dating someone long enough to really have established a personal connection and made a mark on each other's lives—to the point that *not* dating him will mean a noticeable difference in your everyday life, rather than simply a *discontinuation* of something—you definitely owe it to him to tell him face-to-face. Because getting dumped sucks, and the least you can do is have the balls to tell him in person, so that in some small way, it sucks for both of you, not just the person on the receiving end of the email.

THE FADEOUT: WHEN IT HAPPENS TO YOU

THE FADEOUT is an amazing option for breaking up with someone—unless, of course, the fadeout happens to you. Then it's awful. Then it's a drawn-out, terrible period of you wondering if maybe he's just "really busy," and maybe he'll turn up again with apologies and a damned good excuse, and maybe he lost his phone, as well as all access to the Internet. This is followed by a confusing period where you find yourself going over your last date, your last conversation, minute by minute. He *said,* "See you later"! Was he *lying?* Did he know then that he had no intention of actually seeing you later? *Was this his plan all along?!* You'll consider messaging him, demanding that he give you an answer. At least you'd have peace of mind. You'll fantasize about running into him at a bar, where you'd pretend to barely remember his name. In the end, you sort of just get over it. You got faded out. It sucked. But dating karma, man. He who fades out will get faded out, too.

How to
END IT WITH SOMEONE AFTER...

ONE OR TWO DATES

If he asks you out again and you know you don't want to see him, politely turn down the date by saying, "I had a nice time getting to know you, but I'm not sure there's a spark." Or you can just ignore it. He'll get the hint.

A FEW WEEKS

If you've been dating for a few weeks—long enough to have seen each other five or six times, possibly had sex, but *not* met each other's friends—then you can probably get away with an email or a phone call explaining that you're sorry, but things aren't going to work out.

A FEW MONTHS

Break up in person. I know, I know—the last thing you want to do is look at his little face when you tell him it's over. But when you've been dating that long, you really do owe him the courtesy of a face-to-face conversation (and, assuming you're ending on good terms, a goodbye hug!).

ARE YOU BEING TOO PICKY?

ONE OF the major issues that modern daters who are looking for a permanent relationship face is trying to determine who is "the one." An active dater will go on numerous dates a year and will probably have a few relationships under her belt by the time she hits thirty.

So at what point do you stop looking and start settling down? How do you know if you're being too picky, or if you should keep searching for the right person?

A theory developed by Peter Todd, professor of informatics and cognitive science at Indiana University, suggests that the trick is to date enough people to establish some baseline standards, then settle down with the next person you meet who exceeds the bar.

According to Todd's research, **twelve seems to be the magic number when it comes to figuring out what you want in a relationship.** After dating twelve people, most people have enough information to determine what qualities they're looking for in a long-term partner. Statistically speaking, that's the point when people who want to settle down should basically end their search and settle with the next person they date who meets (or surpasses!) these expectations.

In other words . . .

If you've dated fewer than twelve people, feel free to keep looking (and dating).

If you've dated, say, thirty people, you're probably being too picky.

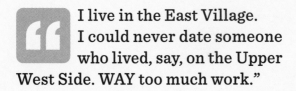

I live in the East Village.
I could never date someone
who lived, say, on the Upper
West Side. WAY too much work."

—Cassie, 34, New York City

Essential
BREAKUP EQUIPMENT

Breakups are the worst, the worst, the worst. Luckily, you can get by with a little help from your friends. And by friends, I mean ice cream, Netflix Instant, and alcohol. We asked women what items they found essential to recovering from a breakup. Here are some of our favorite answers.

- Rom-coms (*The Notebook, Bridget Jones's Diary, In Her Shoes*)
- running shoes
- Kleenex

✳ *plane ticket out*

- Mom
- treadmill
- jersey sheets
- new bra
- chocolate

✳ *beer*

- DVR
- friends to tell you how wonderful you are on command

✳ *credit card*

- Netflix
- exercise
- Gchat
- sappy folk singer of your choice
- comfy pajamas

✳ *delivery*

- thrillers
- whiskey
- a rebound guy

✳ *karaoke*

- ramen
- pizza

- champagne
- a fluffy bathrobe
- new playlists
- Diet Coke

✳ trashy novels •

- the "unfriend" button on Facebook
- frozen yogurt
- Harry Potter

✳ vibrator •

- a hot new boy toy
- confidence
- an Anthropologie dress purchased at full price
- fabulous makeup
- dancing

✳ mascara •

- tea
- tequila, limes, and salt
- John Cusack movies

✳ Ben & Jerry's •

- angry rock music
- bed
- a haircut
- Chapstick

- at least two days to wallow
- a self-help book to tell you how awesome you are
- bike rides
- James Franco

✳ bubble baths •

- cleaning supplies
- Milky Way candy bars
- a make-out session with someone you don't have feelings for
- EXTRA-dirty martinis
- *Pride and Prejudice*

✳ cigarettes •

- Snuggie
- a breakup mix
- a gun, a shovel, and an alibi
- Rilke's *Letters to a Young Poet*
- wine
- guys to sleep with

✳ my cat •

- my dog
- brightly colored lipstick
- a comfy pair of heels that make you feel fabulous

Chapter 6

SEX

———

THE FIRST TIME

(With Someone New)

Once upon a time, being unattached meant that you could pass your whole life without ever knowing what sex was like. You could die a virgin. Untouched. Unsullied. Unorgasmed.

THANK GOD we live in 2012, when the average woman between the ages of eighteen and forty has had around twelve sexual partners (see page 172). Credit feminism, credit *Sex and the City,* credit the magical little pill someone invented to keep you from getting pregnant: Single women are finally allowed to enjoy premarital sex (mostly) without stigma.

But this doesn't mean that we've quite caught up to men yet in terms of sexual equality. Because our sexual freedom was hard-fought and only relatively recently bestowed, women are faced with a new set of pressures. Now that we're (finally!) encouraged to have sex, we worry whether we are having enough of it. Whether we're having too much. Whether

we look a certain way, or act in bed the way other women do. Whether a guy will think less of us if we have sex sooner, whether he will walk away if we wait till later. Many women tend to still be under the impression that there is a "norm" in terms of female sexuality, and they spend far too much time trying to adjust their own sexual habits closer to the median. *Sex and the City,* the same television show that helped make it okay for women to admit that they *have* and *enjoy* sex, constantly depicted the female protagonists huddled around a brunch table, comparing stories and experiences: *Is this normal? Are you doing this too? Is this what men expect?* For women, it hardly ever seems like a simple question of "Yes, I want this" or "No, I don't."

So here's an important question to ask yourself: Do you feel in charge—I mean completely and totally in control—of your own sex life?

Being in control of your own sex life means that you have sex when you're ready. If you're ready on the first date, you go ahead, without worrying that he'll think less of you, without feeling guilty the next morning or telling yourself you should have waited. It means that if you're not ready to have sex by the third date, by the tenth date, by the fifteenth, then you *don't*. And you don't worry about his expectations, you don't make up excuses about why he can't come over, you don't sound overly apologetic about the fact that you just don't *want* to, yet. He'll deal. I can't stress this enough: *You* are the only person who gets to decide when *you* have sex and when *you* don't. Your opinion is the only one that matters.

Being in control of your own sex life means that you are responsible for your health. You have condoms. You go to the doctor. You get checkups. You get tested. You don't take risks.

Being in control of your own sex life means that you get to use your body the way *you* want to. If you wax or shave, it's because that's *your* aesthetic preference, and not because you feel pressure to adhere to a standard of beauty. If you're only doing it because you're worried a guy will be disappointed or unattracted to you if you don't, then save yourself the money and the discomfort. (And he *won't* be disappointed or unattracted; he'll be thrilled to be having sex.) Either way: your body, your sexual experience, your decision.

Being in control of your own sex life means you're as loud or as quiet or as nasty or as prudish in bed as you want to be. You don't

settle for bad sex. You ask for what you want. If you're unhappy with your sex life, you take steps to make it better.

But perhaps most important, being in control of your sex life means being perfectly attuned to your emotions surrounding sex. Because they can fluctuate. It's not like we, as women, adopt an attitude toward sex that stays the same from year to year, and guy to guy. There are slutty periods, there are prudish periods, there are times when it's safe for us to have sex with reckless abandon and times when it isn't. Listen to yourself, check in with yourself, and learn to trust yourself to make the right decisions.

It's time for women to put themselves firmly and irrevocably in the driver's seat of their own sex lives. And then we can *really* enjoy it, completely on our own terms.

Because if we're being really super-honest here, isn't sex, or at least the possibility of sex, one of the most exciting parts about dating? (Yes. Yes, it is.)

According to an ABC News poll, about 29% of Americans say

it's okay to have sex on the first date.

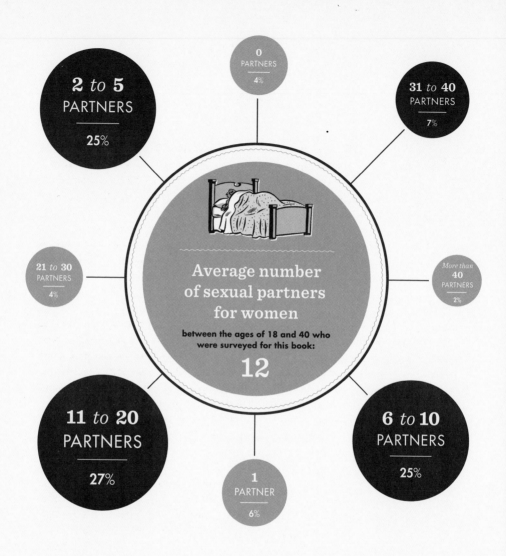

0
PARTNERS
4%

2 *to* **5**
PARTNERS
25%

31 *to* **40**
PARTNERS
7%

21 *to* **30**
PARTNERS
4%

Average number
of sexual partners
for women

between the ages of 18 and 40 who
were surveyed for this book:

12

More than
40
PARTNERS
2%

11 *to* **20**
PARTNERS
27%

6 *to* **10**
PARTNERS
25%

1
PARTNER
6%

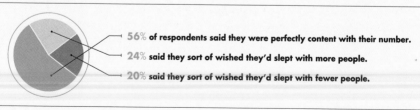

56% of respondents said they were perfectly content with their number.

24% said they sort of wished they'd slept with more people.

20% said they sort of wished they'd slept with fewer people.

WHEN TO HAVE SEX

WE COVERED one-night stands in Chapter 1, which is just to say that this book does not believe in elapsed time as a prerequisite for having sex. If you meet someone, want to have sex with him right away, and feel like it's safe both physically and emotionally for you to do so, go forth and prosper. (Just don't multiply! Yet!)

But sex within a romantic context is different from just sex for sex's sake. When you're dating someone, there are more factors to your relationship than just sex, so deciding when to have sex with someone you're seeing becomes a bit more of a loaded question.

There is a prevalent and *persistent* school of thought that if a woman has sex with a man right away, he won't take her seriously as a potential long-term romantic partner. (Why buy the cow when you can get the milk for free, etc., etc.) Do I even have to outline how sexist this is? How *dare* a guy think less of you for engaging in an activity in which *he is also participating?* You should never feel pressured to "hold off" on sex for fear of losing a guy's respect or ruining your chances of a long-term relationship. After all, you don't lose interest or respect for guys just because they "give in" to having sex with you, do you?

Another prevalent and, frankly, damaging theory floating around is this idea that all men want to have sex all the time, at any cost. Don't get me wrong: Guys really like sex. A lot. Maybe sometimes even more than women do. But they are humans, not just vessels of hormones. If a guy you're dating doesn't seem to want to immediately have sex with you, there is *no need to panic.* It might be unheard-of in pop culture, but it is possible for the *guy* to want to wait until he's ready.

In fact, when you're dating someone with whom you think you have potential for a serious relationship, there is a good case to be made for holding off. By waiting to have sex, both you and your partner are sending a firm message: You're interested in each other physically but *also* emotionally. It's *not* just about sex. And when you *do* have sex, it will be with the understanding that you've established an intimate emotional connection long before establishing a physical one. There's nothing wrong with meaningless sex, but if you're looking for a relationship, you don't want the sex to be meaningless. So it makes sense to wait.

Of course there are tons and tons of long-term couples who had sex on the first date. There are no hard-and-fast rules. Do whatever works best for you.

A Sex Life

WELL LIVED

There is no "normal" when it comes to having sex. It's a weird, funny, natural, awkward, mutable human activity, and no two pairs will have sex the exact same way. Worrying too much about what other people are doing behind closed doors will just prevent you from relaxing into your own brand of sex life.

BUT OF COURSE, it's natural to be a *little* curious in regard to what others are doing in bed, and given that sex is one of the most universal activities on the planet—people from Raleigh to Rome to Riyadh engage in it—there's bound to be some sort of rough baseline of experience. And while so much of sex is about very basic intuition (I mean, you put two people in a room together and they'll figure it out eventually...), there are some practical matters to contend with. Cost, expectations, and the etiquette of sex—these are all things that you should be informed about when you embark upon a dating life.

Keeping in mind that there really is a ton of variation from person to person and couple to couple, here is a very basic look at what a happy, healthy sex life is looking like these days.

ON ORGASMS

IS IT ABSOLUTELY essential that you have an orgasm when you have sex with someone? No, not strictly. But it's pretty important to remember that, ultimately, an orgasm *is* the end goal.

Orgasms aren't the only component to sex, but they're definitely a great component. And while it's not important (or, for some women, even likely) to have an orgasm every time you have sex, an orgasm during partner sex is a goal worth striving for.

If you have trouble loosening up, and you know it, then that's one thing. But if you find yourself ending things prematurely, or worse, faking it, just because you're self-conscious or worried that it's taking too long, you're getting yourself into a bad pattern. You gotta prioritize your own enjoyment as much as your partner's! (Has it ever happened to you that a guy is doing, I don't know, *something* to you, and in your head you're like, *Ugh, that is never, ever going to work,* but instead of correcting him, you pick the easy way out and either fake it or switch tactics or gently end things early, because at this point it doesn't even seem that worth it? Yeah, me too, but we *have to stop doing that!*)

If he gets to come, you get to come. That's just the deal with sex. Don't worry about how long it takes, or how loud you're being, or what your face looks like when you're close, or whether you're sucking in your stomach, or whether he'll want to watch another episode of *Arrested Development* when you're done, or whether his jaw

hurts, or any of the little thoughts that can get between a woman and an orgasm.

And maybe it won't happen this time. That's cool. You probably still had a nice time trying. And you set an important precedent: Your sexual enjoyment is a pursuit worth dedicating time and effort to.

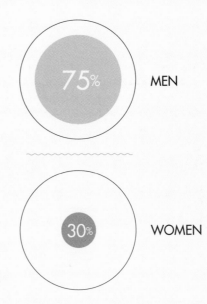

MEN

WOMEN

75% of men say they "always" have an orgasm, while only 30% of women say they do.

TIPS FOR MANAGING YOUR SEXPECTATIONS

CLAIRE CAVANAH *and* RACHEL VENNING,
Co-founders, Babeland

---

1. Check yourself.
Get clear about what you want from sex emotionally, so that you're not surprised by how vulnerable you get. Stay connected to yourself, check in with yourself, and just go as far as you want to go while considering your own emotional readiness.

2. Anything can happen, and whatever happens is okay.
It could be that you have an immediate sexual chemistry and it's great. Or maybe it's only pretty good, but he's open to doing the things you want to do. Or it could be like a comedy of errors. But if you keep lighthearted and positive about it, then it's just sex. You can enjoy whatever the encounter brings.

3. It's totally normal not to orgasm.
Women often don't have orgasms when they have sex with a person for the first time. As you get to know a person and his sexual response and his body—and as that person gets to know you—that's when you're more likely to get all the way there.

4. Do your homework ahead of time.
If you masturbate on your own, you will probably have a much better idea of what turns you on. You'll get in touch with your own body and with what kind of sounds you make, so you won't surprise yourself later on. If you are prepared and know what turns you on, and you know what orgasm feels like for you, then you are much more likely to have a good sexual connection with another person.

5. Don't get discouraged if it's disappointing at first.
Sex really can be worked on, and it does get better with time and communication.

6. Use positive reinforcement.
Instead of saying, "That is way too fast or hard," say, "I really like when you use light pressure; it really turns me on, so let's do more of that." Explain everything as positively as you can, especially in the beginning, because it sets the tone.

7. Sex is more than just intercourse.
Making out, sexy talk, foreplay—what's the hurry to get to intercourse when there's so much other fun to have? Don't expect to get straight down to it every time.

8. Don't prioritize his needs over yours.
You have to stay connected to yourself. You are 50 percent of this, and what you do and say matters. You should be your own best advocate at all times.

HOW MANY CHANCES
should you give after bad sex?

You've gone on a few dates, you definitely like the person, you're attracted to him, you're ready to have sex, and then it's . . . awful. Not "meh" sex, not "it was fine for me" sex, but, like, so bad that you find yourself cringing *while the sex is still happening*. Do you give him another chance? Or is it one strike, he's out? According to a How-AboutWe poll . . .

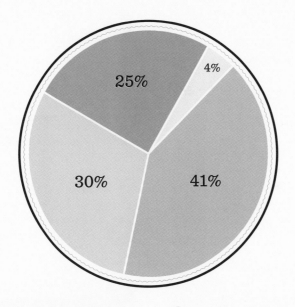

25%

4%

30%

41%

One more shot— but it *has to be good* the next time.	**I'm willing to work on bad sex if the other person is otherwise perfect.**
Two more if I really like someone, but three strikes and he's out.	**Zero! Are you kidding? Life is too short for bad sex.**

The Price of a SEX LIFE

Sex shouldn't cost a thing, and yet, weirdly, we spend money on it! Here's a breakdown:

WHAT IT COSTS TO BE A SEXUALLY ACTIVE WOMAN PER YEAR

BIRTH CONTROL (WITHOUT INSURANCE)
$1,689.87 ($129.99 a pack, 13 packs per year)

+

WAXING
$315 ($35 per waxing, 9 times per year)

+

SHAVING
$191.40 ($15.95 for shaving products per month, 12 times per year)

+

URINARY-TRACT–INFECTION REMEDIES
$48.81 ($40 per prescription of generic antibiotics, plus $8.81 per 32-ounce bottle of all-natural cranberry juice, once a year)

+

LINGERIE
$100 (total spent per year)

+

CONDOMS
$35.98 ($17.99 per box of 36 at Drugstore.com, 2 boxes per year)

+

TOOTHPASTE
$27.93 ($3.99 per tube, 7 tubes per year)

= TOTAL: **$2,408.99**

WHAT IT COSTS TO BE A SEXUALLY ACTIVE MAN PER YEAR

CONDOMS
$35.98 ($17.99 per box of 36 at Drugstore.com, 2 boxes per year)

+

TOOTHPASTE
$27.93 ($3.99 per tube, 7 tubes per year)

= TOTAL: **$63.91**

POSSIBLE VARIABLES:

EMERGENCY CONTRACEPTION (WITHOUT INSURANCE)
$50 (per use, once a year)

+

PREGNANCY TEST
$15 (per test, once a year)

= TOTAL: **$65.00**

NOTE: Any money spent toward bettering your sex life—lingerie! toys! waxing! birth control!—is money well spent, *provided* that it is directly giving you a safer/more pleasurable experience. Otherwise, it's a waste.

The YES/NO/MAYBE List

Another great tip from the experts at Babeland (see also page 176) is to work with your partner to come up with a list of sexual things, then each indicate which of them you would definitely do, might do, and absolutely wouldn't do—like public sex, for example. If public sex is on your "yes" list and his "maybe" list, you can probably make it happen. But if it's a hard "no" for him, you may be out of luck, unless he changes his mind or you move on to a different guy. The following is a (fairly tame) starter list to work from.

* **Blindfolds**

* *Bondage*

* **Cybersex**

* *Dancing*

* **Dominance/ submission**

* *Exhibitionism*

* **Keeping a sex journal**

* *Lap dancing*

* **Massage**

* *Oils/lotions*

* **Outdoor sex**

* *Phone sex*

* **Public sex**

* *Reading erotica*

* **Role-playing**

* *Shaving*

* **Spanking**

* *Stripping*

* **Swinging**

* *Talking dirty*

* **Threesome**

* *Videotaping*

* **Voyeurism**

* *Watching porn*

ROOMMATE SEX ETIQUETTE

IT IS YOUR inalienable right to have sex in your own home, and no roommate can take that away from you. But for a home life that's as happy as your sex life, a little consideration for the folks living with you is in order.

✳ No one apart from the person having sex with you should be able to hear you having sex.

It *is* physically possible to have sex quietly. Save the gratuitous moaning and enthusiastic exclamations for a time when your roommate isn't home. If you really have to have sex in your room while people are around, at least turn on some loud music or a movie to muffle any extraneous sounds.

Of course, slipups do happen. You might not be aware that a roommate is home, or you might get so caught up in the moment that you forget to be quiet. Hopefully your roommate will just slip on some headphones and let it slide. Remember to do the same for him or her if the situation is ever reversed.

✳ Also, no one who isn't currently having sex with you should see you having sex.

For God's sake, *close the door* if you're having sex. Just do it. And while it's an unspoken agreement that while roommates are out of town, you are allowed to have sex on nearly every surface of the home, you should leave no evidence of this, and certainly refrain

from doing so if there's any possibility of your roommate's coming home unexpectedly.

✳ On shower sex:

Do whatever you want in the shower, but *not* when someone else is waiting to use the bathroom for non-recreational purposes (like getting ready for work in the morning).

✳ Alert your roommate to the fact that you have a guest.

If you bring someone home, especially if it's a stranger, try your best to let your roommate know so she isn't caught unawares in her pajamas and hair rollers or what-have-you. It's not imperative that you do so, but it's definitely polite.

✳ Have an old-school signal.

If you're in your room with someone, try to figure out a subtle signal to alert your roommate to this fact (keys in the door? a rubber band?) so she doesn't come knocking on your door at an inopportune moment.

✳ Remember, do unto others . . .

It's up to both of you—you *and* your roommate—to be respectful of each other's sex lives. You're both adults, and you're not living in a convent: Sex is going to happen. Be respectful when you're having sex, and try not to begrudge your roommate too much when it's her turn. If worse comes to worst, always have a pair of headphones nearby.

HE ASKED ME NOT TO SHOWER

"Second date with a guy. (We'd already been out once;
we'd already had sex.) A few hours before the date, I get a text from him:
'Don't shower.' Weird??? Or sort of hot?"

—CLARE, 25, PORTLAND, OREGON

Pre–second date texting exchanges should still be along the lines of "Hope you like Indonesian food!" and "Running 15 min late!"— *not* "Please don't shower in anticipation of having sex with me." Just because you've had sex *once* doesn't mean you're like, *intimate* yet, you know?

Whether it's "sort of hot" is completely up to you, of course. Obviously something can be totally weird and inappropriate and also sexy at the same time.

Finally, an anecdote: Napoleon famously sent his wife Josephine a letter saying, "Coming home in three days: *don't wash.*"

So, there IS a historical precedent for this sort of thing. If that makes a difference to you.

SEXTING:

EVERYTHING YOU WANTED TO KNOW

but Had Too Much Integrity to Ask

Sometimes I think about how we would explain sexting to famous sex luminaries of the past—say, Alfred Kinsey, or the Marquis de Sade. "It's *sort* of like sex, but instead of touching each other, you just write what you'd be doing to each other in a series of short, poorly punctuated messages."

O UR ANCESTORS would be forgiven for thinking that we're absolutely crazy for sexting, but the truth is, as goofy as it sounds, engaging in a licentious exchange with someone you trust can be a great way to perk up a boring Tuesday night (or business trip, or workday, or train ride . . .).

Yes, sexting is here to stay, and with good reason: It's an incredibly efficient form of extended foreplay, and a great way for couples to try out new concepts and keep things interesting.

A lot of the same rules of 3-D sex apply: Do it with someone you're comfortable with, start slowly, respect boundaries, and pay attention to cues from the other person. And the big one: Enjoy it! Yeah, it's completely silly, but so are most sexual acts, when you take a moment to think about them objectively.

THE ART OF THE SEXT (AND YES, IT IS AN ART)

❊ **How to Initiate**

Have you had sex with this person before? If so, you have an easy in: "I can't stop thinking about [last time the two of you had sex]." The obvious rejoinder to this is something along the lines of "Oh, yeah?" or "Me, too, especially [___]," and the conversation sort of flows from there.

If you haven't had sex with this person before, try bringing up sex in general—the topic has a way of going from the broad to the specific when two people are attracted to each other. If you're going to see each other at some point soon, you can coyly text him about how excited you are for your date. A more to-the-point but not explicit thing would be to text him and say, "lying in bed, thinking of you . . . ," or "reading in bed, wish you were here. . . ."

❊ **Delete Delete Delete**

The risk you take when you sext, regardless of who your partner is, is that Gchats and emails and texts can be copied and pasted and forwarded to a third party—or merely casually seen by someone who happens to look at your phone/computer. Erase when you're done!

❊ **Start Slowly, Work Your Way Up**

Dirty talk does not come naturally to everyone, but this doesn't mean you can't still be good at

sexting! In fact, you may find you're able to say things in a text that you can't quite get yourself to say in person—and your partner will definitely think this is hot. Start slowly (the metaphor is your friend!), and then work yourself up to whatever language/level of description you feel comfortable with.

❊ **Just as in Real Sex, There Are Boundaries**

Sexting is a great way for new couples to feel out sexual chemistry, and for long-term couples to explore new ideas in a safe manner. But a sext is not the way to introduce a potentially controversial fetish or topic without having first broached the subject, however lightly, in person.

❊ **Pay Attention to Tone**

You want to sort of match what the other person is doing, and match his tone/pace/wording as much as possible. In all forms of writing and all forms of sex, *transitions* are key!

❊ **It's Only Hot If You Actually Enjoy It**

The important thing is to be playful and actually enjoy yourself. If you're having fun, that will translate through the texts. If you're following a script, or only doing it because you feel like you should, it's not going to be much fun for either of you.

ON NAKED PICTURES AND HOW TO SEND THEM

I'M NOT going to mince words: Taking and sending naked/provocative pictures of yourself is a bad idea. A *terrrrrrible* idea! What you're doing, literally, is creating a digital image of yourself that can be copied, pasted, forwarded, posted, tweeted, and saved forever and ever.

I have naked pictures in my Gmail archives of people I *barely* know. People who would be horrified to know I have seen them naked. But

they took a pic once, and sent it to an ex, who sent it to a friend, who sent it to a friend, who sent it to me, and now, if I wanted to, I could keep it forever.

I know a guy who has a creepy folder on his computer that contains photographs of at least six different girls he's slept with and (somehow!) conned into sending him pics. This guy isn't ever going to *do* anything with these photographs, but ugh, isn't it gross to know he *has* them and can look at them whenever he wants to, long after the women have stopped sleeping with him?

Your naked body is a sight to behold . . . in person. Don't give someone the option of being able to queue it up as easily as an episode of *Frasier* on Netflix Instant.

But.

But.

Obviously, as human beings, we aren't perfectly rational all the time. Obviously, in the heat of the moment, one can't be blamed for failing to think of every possible ramification. And obviously, the allure of sending someone a sexy picture is strong—otherwise, *surely* politicians, actors, and public figures, who have the most at stake, would be able to refrain from sending them.

So if you're going to send naked pictures, at least be careful about it. And at least make them flattering.

How to Take

FLATTERING NAKED PICTURES

WITHOUT LOSING YOUR DIGNITY

1

DON'T INCLUDE YOUR FACE

If your face is in the pic, then there's no denying that the photo is of you. Crop it out! (And let's be real: If you're taking naked pictures in the first place, then your face is not the important part.)

2

LIGHTING IS KEY

Candlelight = super-flattering. Shadows = slimming. Overhead light in bathroom = No. No. No.

3

PUT A LITTLE ART INTO IT

You don't need to, like, set up a tableau or drape yourself à la *Grande Odalisque*, but do at least take into account the background of the photograph. A single jar of, I dunno, Vicks VapoRub can undo all the attempted sexiness of your shot.

4

USE TWO MIRRORS

Both Scarlett Johansson and Blake Lively used mirrors to great effect in their own leaked pictures. (See?? It's horrible that I know this! Naked pictures are not safe!) Anyway. Good way to get a 360-degree view, *if that's what you're into.*

5

YOU CAN BE PROVOCATIVE WITHOUT BEING NAKED

If you feel uncomfortable going full-frontal and documenting it for posterity but still want to send a sexy picture, there are ways to do it while still keeping all the important parts covered up. Be cheeky! Show cleavage; show yourself in a sheet; show yourself naked but sitting in a way that covers everything. Or show something that's completely unidentifiable as you, like a nipple.

FIVE THINGS TO SAY WHILE SEXTING

———

A S WITH MOST things in the sex-and-romance department, nearly everything sounds super-cheesy when you're not "in the moment" and are just reading the line in a book. And when you *are* "in the moment," even the dumbest, cheesiest lines can work.

With that in mind, here are a few fail-safes to get you started if you lack inspiration. . . .

1. *"Can't stop thinking about last night."*

2. *"Getting ready for bed, wish you were here to help me fall asleep . . . . "*

3. *"What are you thinking about right now . . . ?"*

4. *"Here's what I would do if you were with me right now . . . ."*

5. *"What are you wearing?"* *(Cheesy, funny; he'll get the point.)*

In a poll conducted by U.K.-based mobile news site Recombu of 2,000 adults, 47% of respondents said

they send sexts to their significant others.

Of that group, about 11% have mistakenly sent sexts to the wrong person.

~~~~~~~~~~

Men are more likely than women to accidentally send sexts to someone else.

16% of men have sent one to a family member and 8% of women have done the same.

THINKING ABOUT SENDING A DIRTY PIC?

☒ ***Read this first:***

☐ 1. You're sending this picture to someone with whom you have a sexual relationship of some sort. (No unsolicited dirty pictures!)

☐ 2. You are *not* sending it to a boss, an employee, a stranger, or someone who is needlessly casual with his phone/email passwords.

☐ 3. No one else has access to your phone/computer.

☐ 4. You have no interest in running for office someday.

☐ 5. You are totally at peace with the idea that your recipient could keep this photo of you for the rest of his life.

☐ 6. You are completely fine with the possibility that friends/strangers/vague acquaintances might see these photos.

☐ 7. If your mother somehow got her hands on these photos, it would not be the end of the world.

☐ 8. Did you say yes to *every single one* of these? Fine! Go ahead. Snap away. You're only young once.

23%

A New York *Daily News* survey reported that 23% of women

have been photographed or filmed naked.

The Worst-Case Scenario

SEX-SURVIVAL GUIDE

WHAT IF:

{ You Haven't Shaved? }

{ His Penis Is Too Big? }

{ He's Bad at Going Down on You? }

{ He "Can't" Wear a Condom? }

{ You or Your Partner Has an STD? }

{ He Won't Go Down on You? }

* Did *he* remember to shave? Okay, well, just saying.
* Make up for what you lack in smooth skin with unbridled enthusiasm. (He is *never* going to notice a little stubble, and a tuft of hair won't bother him.)
* Grab a razor, pull him into the bathroom, and make it part of your foreplay.

* Not everyone likes oral. It's fine if he doesn't like giving *or* receiving. But he can't expect you to go down on him if he doesn't go down on you. Right? That's just obvious.
* Bring it up to him. Maybe he's just inexperienced? Maybe he's had a bad experience with it in the past? Maybe it just seriously didn't occur to him?
* If performing oral is a deal-breaker for him, then you need to figure out if not receiving it is a deal-breaker for you. (And it's okay if the answer is yes! There are lots of guys out there who would be more than happy to spend some time down there.)

* TELL HIM. You're a responsible, sexually active adult. You have to tell him. And you have to ask, every time you have sex with someone new: "Hey, before we get too carried away, I gotta let you know that I have _____, but I'm taking ___, and it's totally safe as long as we use a condom."
* There are *lots* of different ways to have sex that don't involve penetration. Toys, foreplay, ___. Get creative!

* Don't get too freaked out! Your body is probably more able to cope with a large size than you realize, but fear/nerves can cause you to tense up, which makes sex harder.
* Take things slowly, focus on foreplay, and don't start intercourse until you're absolutely ready. (You may need to use additional lubricant.)
* Stick to positions in which you can control the speed/depth of penetration (such as you on top).

* Use delicate, positive reinforcement! Be vocal about what you like, and gentle about what you don't like.
* Show him what you want, instead of just telling him. (*How* you decide to show him is up to you.)
* Be patient. Don't give up on him! You are teaching him a very useful, rewarding skill.

* Bullshit. Come on. It might be less pleasurable to wear condoms, but that's no reason to compromise on your safety. Unless you're in an exclusive relationship, he needs to wear a condom while having intercourse with you. That's *your* deal-breaker.

You Want to Have
Sex in Public?

He's Too Rough?

He Doesn't Want to
Have Sex Very Often
(or as Often as You Do)?

You're on Your
Period?

His Penis Is Small?

The Condom Breaks?

One of You Is Signifi-
cantly Overweight?

He's Not Rough
Enough?

* Stop having sex *immediately* when you notice the condom is broken.
* Go get Plan B as soon as possible. It's perfectly okay to ask him to split the cost with you—it's HIS potential baby that you're opting to not conceive!
* Get tested at the next possible opportunity. Just in case.

* Be open, and talk about it when you aren't too emotional. Listen to what he has to say. It may be a case of just having different sex-drive levels, in which case communication between the two of you is key to finding a balance that's satisfying for both.

* TELL him you're on your period! If you're fine with having sex anyway, and he's fine too, then proceed!
* Put a towel down, or use a diaphragm to make things less messy. Or have sex in the shower!
* It's still possible to get pregnant on your period, so never use period sex as an excuse to forgo a condom!

* Do it! Why not? There are more harmful ways to get your kicks than that.
* If you're nervous about it, you can start somewhere where the risk of being caught is relatively low (like when you're camping in the woods), and slowly escalate (in a parked car!) until you're ready for the big time (in a bar bathroom or something).

* Put the brakes on, and tell him to stop. Don't just let it happen if you're feeling uncomfortable pain, or he accidentally leaned on your hair funny, or he's spanking you.
* Sometime before the next time you have sex, maybe have a conversation about what you're okay with in bed and what you're not. Boundaries, man!

* Communicate about it beforehand. If your partner is the one who's overweight, he probably has experience navigating sex and will be able to tell you what's possible and what isn't.

* Tell him what you like! Some guys are (understandably) timid when it comes to hair-pulling/pinning down. Make it clear that it's okay with you!
* Set clear boundaries. If you tell him what's going too far, that takes out the guesswork, and he can feel more comfortable with everything below the line.

* Focus on foreplay as much as possible, and find positions that sort of, you know, make the most of what he's got. (From behind, for example.)
* If you really like the guy, don't let something like this be a deal-breaker. Buy a dildo! Get creative! Figure out a way to make your sex life satisfying for both of you.

Chapter 7

THE FIRST
SIX MONTHS

———

Are You Ready for
A RELATIONSHIP?

Every once in a while, everything will go right. The first date, the second date, the third. The conversation is good, the sex is good, the level of communication is just how you like it. Things are moving along so nicely, in fact, that one day (maybe sooner rather than later, maybe later rather than sooner), you realize: *Yeah, I don't really want to date anyone else right now. I'm good with just this person.* And then (provided your partner feels the same way), you move into relationship territory.

T HE FIRST SIX months of a new relationship are unlike any other. You're in the honeymoon phase, that hazy, cozy period of time where you'd be perfectly content to forget the other billion-something inhabitants on the planet. You wake up some mornings and can't really believe your luck when you confirm that he's on the pillow next to you. You feel slightly bad for your single friends, because they're alone, and for your coupled-up friends, because

their significant others are so clearly lacking in comparison to yours. You find ways to drop the word *boyfriend* into conversations whenever possible, and you get a secret thrill every time you say it. Every moment of the year is a landmark—the holidays, Valentine's Day, summer—because last year you were single, and this year you are together. You delight in exploring this newfound identity of two-some—of defining what your restaurants are, your songs, your routines.

> **With my boyfriend, it was never a question. I knew we were both interested, and I knew we would see each other again. Which is crazy, 'cause there was always that question with previous guys."**
>
> —Beth, 25, Boston

Yes, the reason people who are newly in relationships can be so noxiously happy is because, quite frankly, there are few things in life that are so patently wonderful. Falling in love—and having that love reciprocated—is arguably the best thing that can happen to a human being. Some people never fall in love at all. If you're lucky enough to have it happen to you, it would be a waste not to relish every last moment of it.

But whereas in romantic comedies the credits roll once the girl finds the guy, in real life, the story continues, and the hero and heroine need to figure out how to be with each other now that they've found each other. A good relationship shouldn't be hard work, but there are still hurdles to cross. How fast is too fast? What will "boyfriend" and "girlfriend" look like for you? How can you lay the groundwork to ensure that you'll still want to be with someone even after the excitement of the first six months wears off?

Take it one day at a time, but prepare yourself for a long (and wonderful, and bumpy, and enriching) road.

DO YOU WANT TO TAKE THINGS
TO THE NEXT LEVEL?

☒ *If you answer "yes" to all of these questions,*
you're probably ready:

☐ 1. Have you stopped seeing other people? (Or, do you like the guy in question enough to stop seeing other people?)

☐ 2. When you meet a cute guy, are you able to register his cuteness without immediately feeling tempted to go after him, or wondering what it would be like to date him instead, or comparing him to your current guy?

☐ 3. Have you stopped signing in to dating sites to check your messages?

☐ 4. Have you talked to your friends about him?

☐ 5. Are you totally over your ex (and most residual feelings of resentment or bitterness regarding your breakup)? (In other words, no unresolved issues.)

According to a study conducted by Facebook,

people who list themselves as
"In a Relationship" are happier than
people who are single.

HOW TO BROACH THE TOPIC OF EXCLUSIVITY

I
F YOU'VE DECIDED you want to go exclusive, the next step is to have a conversation about it. He may or may not agree to it at this time, but talking about it at least puts you guys on the same page in terms of what you want.

Too many girls are afraid of voicing their needs for fear of seeming pushy, in case the guy doesn't feel the same way. Having a conversation isn't pushy, though! It's adult. If you guys each know where the other stands, that leaves little room for game-playing, guessing, or unnecessary drama. If you want a relationship and he doesn't (or vice versa!!), you can make an informed decision about whether to continue to see each other or end things.

When you bring this up for the first time, make sure to do it when you're both relaxed and in a good mood. (Do not bring it up during a fight or a tiff; do not bring it up when one of you is stressed or upset about something else.) You also *miiiiight* want to consider avoiding the ominous "Can we talk?." Those three words tend to put everyone on instant alert, and you want this conversation to be open and relaxed, not tense.

So just, apropos of nothing (or with whatever segue you deem fit), broach the subject.

You've been dating for X amount of time. It's been really great. You're not seeing anyone else, and you don't want to see anyone else. What does he think?

He might just immediately say, "Yes! I don't want to see anyone else either. Let's change our Facebook statuses *right now.*" Which is great and exciting, and you can immediately call your friends and practice referring to him as your boyfriend, which will give you a little thrill each time you say it for at least two weeks.

Or he might say that while he likes you and is having a great time, he's just not ready for a commitment like that yet. He might have a pretty valid reason for feeling this way, and it's great that he's being honest (rather than rushing into something he's not actually ready for). If this happens, then it's up to you to decide what the next move is. If you like him enough and are in no real rush for a relationship, you might consider continuing to date him casually and then checking in again in six months (with the understanding that his answer might be the same). Or, if you're really looking for something serious, it might be time to cut your losses, as great as this guy is, and dedicate your time to finding someone who wants the same things you do.

GOING FOR IT

S O YOU AGREED, and he agreed, and now you're In a Relationship, just like that. But apart from the label, and from the assurance that both of you aren't seeing other people, there's probably not a whole lot that's going to change right away. You're probably going to continue to see each other at relatively the same rate (at least at first), and you're probably still going to talk about each other and interact with each other much in the same way you had been.

But gradually, your relationship will start to evolve, one mini-milestone at a time. Pay attention to the firsts! You only get one go at each of them, and they're kind of sweet, in their own way.

Ten Milestones on the Way to a Serious Relationship:

1. The First Time You Don't Schedule Weekend Plans

That seamless transition between having to wait until Wednesday to ask, "What are you up to this weekend?" and having it be a given that you two are going to hang out.

2. The First Time You Meet Each Other's Friends

This usually happens casually, in the form of meeting up with people for a drink or stopping by a party. But make no mistake: Meeting each other's friends is a big deal.

3. **The First Time You Spend a Night In**
Finally getting to the point where a Friday night can mean takeout and a movie at home, rather than a *date* date.

4. **The First Time You See Each Other "Au Naturel"**
You've probably already seen each other "strategically naked." This means that while technically you've removed your clothing, you still have the aid of sheets, pillows, dim lighting, and natural-looking makeup that you sneakily reapply in the bathroom.

Seeing each other *naked* naked for the first time—unbrushed hair, blotchy skin, stubble and, for women, without makeup—means you're pretty darn comfortable with each other.

5. **The First Time You Call Just to Talk**
Maybe you called about something else, or to schedule a date, or to check up on something. But then, once this information is exchanged, you don't immediately hang up. You find you have lots of things to say to each other, and before you know it, half an hour has gone by. It's not just physical: You two are in serious like.

6. **The First Time You See Each Other Really Drunk**
You accompany him to a party, he overdoes it, you take him home, he gets sick, then sad, then wild, then passes out . . . and you still like him the next morning? It's love.

7. **The First Time You Talk About Your Exes**
Everyone knows not to mention an ex on a first (or second, or third) date, but eventually the subject is bound to come up. Talking about each other's exes and dating histories shows that you care about a person enough to hear all the gory details of his dating life.

8. **Seeing Each Other Sick**
Being sick means feeling tired, vulnerable, crabby, and gross. Letting someone see you when you feel that way (and, conversely, not being turned off by seeing someone that way) is a sign that things are getting serious.

9. **The First Time You Just Go to Sleep**
We've already established that sharing a bed with someone sucks. If you're willingly doing that and you're not even hooking up, you must *really* like each other.

10. **The First Fight**
You're comfortable enough to express frustration with each other—and committed enough to not just walk away. The first time you fight, and survive, you'll know that both of you are committed to seeing where this relationship takes you.

TEN THINGS YOU SHOULDN'T DO
UNTIL YOU'RE EXCLUSIVE

———

WAITING UNTIL you're exclusive to have sex is too old-fashioned a maxim to work for everyone, but there are other things that should happen only after you're committed...

1. Friending each other's friends on Facebook.

2. Staying in each other's bed/apartment after the other leaves for work.

3. Going to each other's work functions.

4. Asking each other to pick up anything remotely health-related (tampons, sinus medicine, birth control, foot cream).

5. Having nights when you stay in and just watch TV.

6. Peeing with the door open. (Or never! Never is also an option for this one!)

7. Introducing each other to your parents.

8. Making plans more than a week or two in advance (i.e., booking concert tickets for three months from now).

9. "Popping by" each other's place of work unexpectedly.

10. Doing each other's laundry.

RELATIONSHIP ADVICE

Every relationship is different and, more to the point, customizable. What worked with your ex won't necessarily work with your current SO (Significant Other). But there are some rules worth sticking to, from relationship to relationship. Below are some examples of tips and observations that these daters have learned from experience.

"Know someone through every season. People wig out during the holidays."

—LAURA, 28, CHICAGO

"Don't cook or bake for him until you're certain that you want to move forward with him. I put a lot of heart and soul into what I'm cooking or baking, and I don't want to feel like I've wasted the effort on someone who doesn't really care about me."

—BETH, 25, BOSTON

"I never let him see me pee, and I never fart around him, ever."

—SARAH, 26, CHICAGO

"You should not bring anyone to a friend's wedding unless you've known him for five months."

—JOY, 30, PORTLAND, MAINE

"I've always found it to be true that a lesbian relationship gets more intense faster. Along with the hormones thing, maybe there's also the taboo element, since lesbians are still a minority. We feel like we're doing something wrong and we're in it together and it's illicit and beautiful and heart-pulsing—it takes very little time for us to want to spend every second with each other."

—MELANIE, 26, NEW YORK CITY

"Don't feel like you have to do every single thing together. Go out and have your own individual experiences so you have something to talk to each other about."

—LAUREN, 32, BROOKLYN

The
HONEYMOON PHASE

T HE FIRST SIX months of a relationship set the tone for your entire relationship, so communication and honesty are vital. Unfortunately, the first six months are also when people tend to be the most smitten with each other, which means that you might be more willing to let things slide, or more hesitant to speak up about your particular needs or wants.

Things are *lovely* during the early stages, but to ensure that they continue to be lovely, it's so important to really use this time to figure out not only the logistics of dating each other ("How will we act together around our parents?", "Where will we spend most of our time?") but also how you communicate with each other. What you're building right now is a relationship where both people are in tune with each other's needs and really receptive to each other's concerns. So if you think you're spending too much time together, or too little; if you're unsatisfied with something romantically or sexually; if you've got a nagging worry, don't be afraid to voice it.

And don't forget: With every first, you're setting a tone. It sounds cheesy when you're reading it in a book, but really: Have open communication about what kind of relationship you want. It will help things during the first six months, and the six months after that, and after that, and after that . . . .

I HAVEN'T HAD NIGHTTIME SEX IN MONTHS

"My boyfriend has always really liked morning sex, and lately he's
had no interest in evening sex. I'm a girl, and I like my romantic evenings,
plus on work mornings there's always a rush factor, when at night there isn't.
The other thing I think about (which I KNOW is irrational) is, like, come on,
in the morning you WAKE UP . . . ready to go, so to speak . . . you don't
even have to look at me or touch me to get in the mood!"

—LORI, 28, SAN DIEGO

Hmm, Lori, are you guys going on enough dates? If you and your boyfriend go out in big groups and get wasted and stay out till all hours, it totally makes sense for you guys to just sort of crash in bed and deal with romance in the morning—that's natural. Same with the end of a long workday—he may just feel exhausted at night.

It seems like morning sex might be the status quo in your relationship, which really should be fine as long as at least *sometimes* you have more prolonged, romantic sex in the evening, as opposed to the morning quickie.

The best way to deal with this is to make sure to plan romantic dates with each other— just the two of you. Going on romantic dates will rekindle the early, "courtship" phase of your relationship—you'll both get dressed up, the night will feel out of the ordinary, and you'll both be much more likely to end it with sex instead of just crashing. (If you get home after a long romantic evening together and he flips on the TV and says, "Not tonight," he's a jerk.)

Of course, you can always go the unpopular route and *talk* to him about how you feel. Explain that you love morning sex—and afternoon sex and nighttime sex and lunchtime sex. So how about mixing things up a bit?

And the third solution, of course, is to just make it happen. If you initiate, is he really gonna turn it down? Remember, it takes two to tango. He's not the only one to set your sexual routines, so don't be afraid to speak up or take action for what you want.

What to Do
WHEN YOU FIRST MEET...

THE FRIENDS

Smile a Lot

For this first meeting, it's more important to come off as friendly than anything else. You want to seem nice and approachable.

Don't Try to Be the Center of Attention

Engage with them, but don't try to dominate the conversation. Listen to what his friends are saying!

Know That Your SO Might Be Slightly Different Around Different Friends

Yes, it's quite possible that your boyfriend acts one way around you, his girlfriend, and an entirely different way around his buddies. Do not be shocked; do not be appalled.

Don't Try Too Hard

Ultimately, all anyone wants for a friend is someone who is crazy about him and treats him well. All anyone is really looking to see is that you're a good girlfriend.

THE BOSS / CO-WORKERS

Don't Try to Be Buddy-Buddy

Whatever his relationship with his boss and co-workers is, it's probably best to play it safe and err on the side of keeping things professional.

Be Careful How Much You Drink

Do not get drunk. Oh my God, do not get drunk. You will feel embarrassed and awkward at all subsequent work functions.

Be Careful What Information You Reveal

You don't really know what kind of personal information your SO reveals at work, so try to keep to conversation topics that are neutral, i.e., not about yourselves.

Make a Good Impression for Him

When you're meeting friends or siblings or parents, you're the one trying to make a good impression. But when it comes to work functions, he is. So try to be your most charming, relaxed, put-together self.

THE PARENTS

Bring a Gift

Flowers. A box of chocolates. A bottle of wine. Something specific from your hometown or wherever you're coming from. His family will definitely appreciate the gesture.

Dress Your Best!

Dressing up in order to meet someone is a sign of respect. It shows that you care enough about making a good impression to *put in effort*.

Let Your Significant Other Take the Lead Re: Physical Affection

If your SO holds your hand or kisses you in front of his or her parents, then you can go ahead and return the gestures. But don't go in for a kiss in front of the folks without getting the okay.

Stay on Neutral Topics

Stick to those subjects. Anything that you wouldn't feel comfortable talking about on a first date should definitely be avoided when meeting parents. (This includes money, politics, religion, and sex.)

Pitch In

Help with setting the table, washing the dishes, and any little task that needs to be done. Don't ask, "Is there anything I can do to help?"—just jump right in.

THE SIBLINGS

Siblings Are Great PR Reps: Use Them to Your Advantage

Remember, the siblings are connected to everyone else in the family—the parents, grandparents, aunts, uncles, etc. Get them to like you and they'll put in a good word with the rest of the family.

Do Your Research

Before meeting a brother or sister, ask your significant other for some basic info: Is he in school? Does she work? What are his hobbies, etc.? Then you can easily start a conversation by saying, "Sally tells me you breed carrier pigeons?" (or whatever).

Take Cues from Your SO

Pay attention to how your significant other relates to his siblings. Are they affectionate? Do they tease each other? Are they slightly detached? Note the tone of their relationship, and then mimic it to a lesser degree.

Stay Out of Any Sibling Tension

If you sense tension between your boyfriend and his siblings, do your best to stay neutral. Even if your boyfriend doesn't get along with his brother or sister, it's still in your best interest that the sibling likes *you*.

Give Them Space

There's nothing quite like the relationship between brothers and sisters. Respect that. Hang back when necessary: Let them do their thing.

WHO STAYS WHERE?

ONE OF THE trickier aspects of a new relationship is deciding where you're going to spend the majority of your nights together.

If both of you have pretty similar living situations and equidistant work commutes, it probably makes sense to split the nights fairly evenly. Doesn't have to be *exactly* fifty-fifty, but it's nice when both people in the relationship feel equally comfortable at each other's houses and trade off hosting/overnight-bagging duties.

If one person has, like, a significantly nicer living situation than the other, or if one person has roommates and the other person doesn't, then you might decide to spend most of your time at that person's apartment. This is a bit inconvenient for the person stuck perpetually carrying his or her life in an overnight bag (it's sort of like having divorced parents), but on the other hand, he or she gets to enjoy a sweet apartment a few nights a week, so it all works out.

And then there's always the possibility of finding yourself spending most of your together nights at one person's house even though it's *not* significantly nicer or more convenient than the other. This sucks. It basically means that one person is lazy/unwilling

to change up his routine. Not fair! Speak up! You should be sharing the burden of splitting your time between two places.

❋ **When it comes to a new relationship, how much is too much, in terms of spending time together?**

Well, I don't want to sound prescriptive, and every couple is different, but . . . six nights a week. Six nights a week or more together is legitimately too much. You guys just started dating, and as tempting as it might be to spend every waking moment together, it's much better for you (and the future of your relationship) if you temper things, at least in the beginning. The way to ensure long-term happiness in a relationship is to hold on to your own identity. Keep going out with friends, keep doing your own thing, and keep having the occasional night of just browsing the Internet on your couch. Seriously, this will make your relationship better! Because you'll have things to talk about, things to catch up on. Seeing each other will continue to be a high point of your week, rather than just routine. And honestly, you have the rest of your life to be each other's routine! Don't be afraid to ease into things.

Five Things to Have
IN YOUR OVERNIGHT BAG

YOUR MAKEUP
1

**WORK CLOTHES/
GYM CLOTHES**

(for the next day)
4

PILL
if applicable (or any other med)
5

**WHATEVER YOU'RE
READING**
2

**FLAT IRON/HAIR CURLER/
HAIR DRYER**
(alternatively, depending on the state
of his shower, dry shampoo)
3

Five Things to Have
AT HIS PLACE

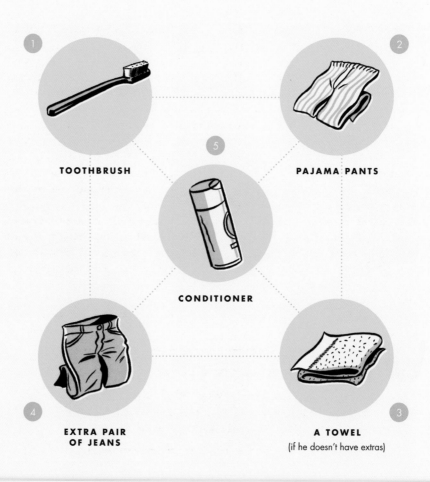

1 TOOTHBRUSH

2 PAJAMA PANTS

5 CONDITIONER

4 EXTRA PAIR
OF JEANS

3 A TOWEL
(if he doesn't have extras)

DOING THE LONG-DISTANCE THING

———

IT SEEMS LIKE there are more reasons than ever for couples to spend extended periods of time apart. It's just part of the conundrum of modern love: No one wants to compromise her love life or her professional life. If you or your significant other gets an opportunity that's hard to pass up, even if it means being far away from each other, you should feel comfortable going for it without feeling like it's at the expense of your relationship.

Personal circumstances can also be a cause of extended absences. And sometimes people from different cities meet and fall in love. If you really feel that you'd rather be with this person than without him, despite the distance, then long-distance is probably worth it.

In many ways, long-distance relationships (let's call them LDRs for short) get a bad rap. Yeah, they're hard. Yeah, it's frustrating not being able to see your boyfriend—one of the most important people in your life—without getting on a plane. And unfortunately, yes, LDRs come with their own unique sets of frustrations and issues that often make relationships harder—sometimes too hard for a couple to withstand.

But honestly? It's not the end of the world, thanks to modern technology and discount airlines. If you're really committed to each other, there's no reason an LDR can't work.

ON MAKING YOURSELF AT HOME

Don't start leaving things at his place before you've been invited to, especially if it's early in the relationship. But if you're spending most of your nights at his place and he doesn't so much as let you leave a toothbrush, bring it up!

FIVE WAYS TO SURVIVE
A LONG-DISTANCE RELATIONSHIP

1. **Make your relationship a priority, and visit each other as much as humanly and financially possible.**

2. **When you're apart, have a specific scheduled time when you talk or catch up.**
It's easy to get into fights or tiffs when you feel disconnected, so regular communication is important!

3. **Always count down to when you'll see each other next, not up.**
"I'll see him in three weeks!" vs. "We've been apart for four weeks now."

4. **Have an end date.**
"Maybe other people can do long-distance and have no idea when it is going to end, but I couldn't. This is maybe controversial advice, but I don't think it's worth it if you don't know when you'll be living in the same place again." —Rachel, 27, New York City

5. **Keep living your life!**
It's tempting, when you're in an LDR, to just live for phone calls/Skype sessions from your SO. But the more you distract yourself with your friends and your life, the faster the time will go. (And the more you'll have to talk about when you talk/see each other again!)

ON LDR SEX:

"Best sex you'll ever have. My therapist says it's because there's a lot of insecurity and because you get so emotional, but I think you're just horny."

—Kristi, 25, Chicago

THE ART OF THE SKYPE DATE

———

NOTHING CAN substitute for actually being with your date and doing something fun with him. But if you're stuck in a long-distance relationship, you can definitely make Skype work for you.

1. **If Possible, Skype Somewhere Private!**
Sometimes people Skype in cafés, which is fine . . . if you want everyone in the café to join you on your date. If at all possible, it's much better to Skype somewhere where you can feel free to talk at length, without a room full of strangers listening.

2. **But If You Are in Public, Have Fun with It!**
One of my friends used to Skype with her boyfriend in a café. They would keep their conversation very PG but type dirty things to each other in the chat box to try to make each other laugh. A fun solution to in-public Skype-ing.

3. **Think of the Cam-er-ah!**
You're basically going to be on camera . . . so use it to your advantage! The perfect lighting for a Skype date is a light behind your monitor and another light on one side. Have your computer level with your eyeline, or even slightly above. If you look down at your computer, it's easy to get a few extra chins. And while Skype-ing, be sure to look at your camera when you talk, and not at your screen/self. It's really obvious when you spend most of the Skype call checking yourself out/fixing your hair/preening instead of being focused on the other person.

4. **Skip Dinner, Have Dessert**
Skype dinner dates are pretty popular for LDRs, but staring at a screen and chewing can be sort of boring/tedious. Maybe plan instead to Skype during dessert, or over post-dinner drinks: much less cutlery and mastication involved, and still participatory.

5. **The Movie Skype Date**
Pick a movie to watch on Netflix or Hulu. Start a Skype video session. Click "Share Screen." Instant movie night!

6. **The All-Nighter**
Leave Skype on all night so you can wake up together, get ready together, and hang out together in the morning. Kind of voyeuristic (especially if you're in different time zones, in which case presumably one person will be awake much sooner and therefore watching the other sleep), but definitely appealing for serious couples.

Should You
MOVE IN WITH HIM?

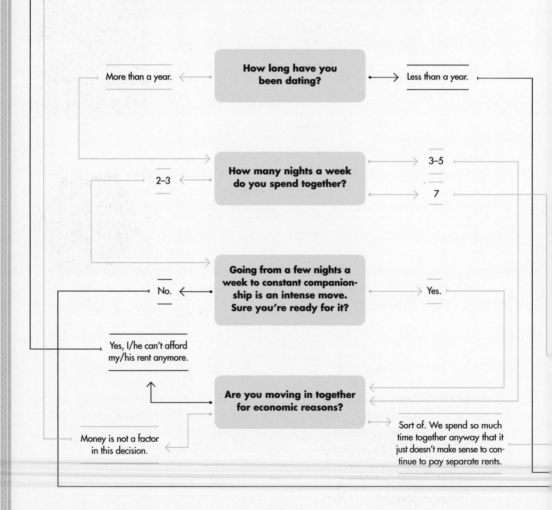

How long have you been dating?

More than a year.   Less than a year.

How many nights a week do you spend together?

2–3   3–5   7

Going from a few nights a week to constant companionship is an intense move. Sure you're ready for it?

No.   Yes.

Yes, I/he can't afford my/his rent anymore.

Are you moving in together for economic reasons?

Money is not a factor in this decision.

Sort of. We spend so much time together anyway that it just doesn't make sense to continue to pay separate rents.

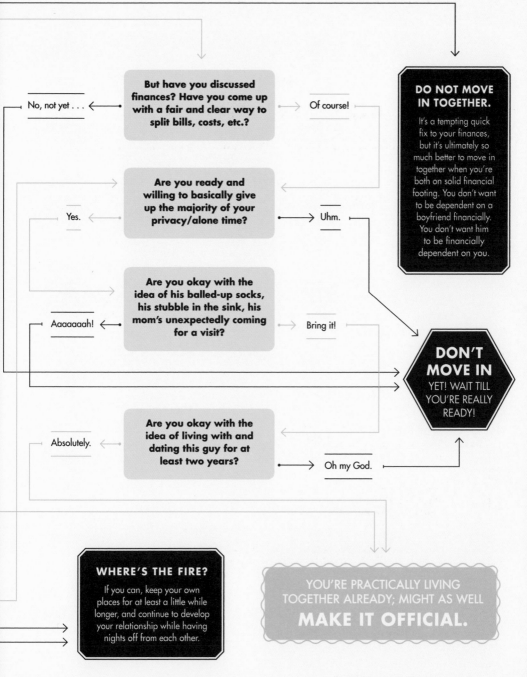

But have you discussed finances? Have you come up with a fair and clear way to split bills, costs, etc.?

No, not yet . . .

Of course!

DO NOT MOVE IN TOGETHER.

It's a tempting quick fix to your finances, but it's ultimately so much better to move in together when you're both on solid financial footing. You don't want to be dependent on a boyfriend financially. You don't want him to be financially dependent on you.

Are you ready and willing to basically give up the majority of your privacy/alone time?

Yes.

Uhm.

Are you okay with the idea of his balled-up socks, his stubble in the sink, his mom's unexpectedly coming for a visit?

Aaaaaaah!

Bring it!

DON'T MOVE IN YET! WAIT TILL YOU'RE REALLY READY!

Are you okay with the idea of living with and dating this guy for at least two years?

Absolutely.

Oh my God.

WHERE'S THE FIRE?

If you can, keep your own places for at least a little while longer, and continue to develop your relationship while having nights off from each other.

YOU'RE PRACTICALLY LIVING TOGETHER ALREADY; MIGHT AS WELL **MAKE IT OFFICIAL.**

THE CONDOM CONVERSATION

PART OF the joy of a relationship is the fact that you don't need to use condoms anymore, right? (Well, you might feel relatively neutral on the matter, but for your boyfriend, it's definitely a perk. One of many perks to dating you, obviously.)

Before you hop off the Trojan horse, make sure you've both gotten tested recently. (You could go together! It could be romantic?) You also might as well take the opportunity to discuss, at least in a cursory sense, your sexual histories. This doesn't need to be an exceptionally detailed account—you don't need to go into names or numbers or anything—but it's a good idea to have at least *some* idea of your partner's sexual past. (Otherwise you'll find out ten years into your marriage, which will cause a midlife marital crisis that will read like the plot of a B movie.)

Once you're on the same page, in terms of each other's sexual past, you should definitely discuss what birth-control option you'll be using. Whether you want him to participate in the discussion of what BC to use is up to you, but he should absolutely be informed as to what specific measures are being taken to prevent a baby in nine months' time.

Should you split the cost of birth control? Totally differs from couple to couple. If you're paying $60 a month for a NuvaRing and strongly feel he should chip in (it's his not-baby, too!), then feel free to bring it up. If you were on birth control before you started dating him and will continue to be on it if you break up, you might just consider it a personal expense. Whatever works best for the two of you.

> " Most guys I've met prefer sex without a condom. But, whatever—it's not like they won't enjoy themselves either way."
>
> —Katie, 34, Seattle

THE IMPORTANCE OF DATE NIGHT

ONE OF THE loveliest things about being in a relationship is that suddenly it becomes okay to hunker down at home together. After all, isn't that sort of the point of having a boyfriend? That you can stop dressing up and dragging yourself to a crowded restaurant, and can instead just luxuriate in sex and happy companionship at home?

Yes, staying home is lovely and comfortable. But continuing to go out on dates is an essential component to a happy relationship. It's *good* for couples to get dressed up once in a while and experience something new together.

Because a boyfriend, a significant other, should be so much more than a roommate you have sex with. You want to establish a dynamic with someone that will continue to be exciting long after the honeymoon phase. You want someone who's going to be a partner in crime, someone with whom you can share a vibrant, exciting, sexy life. Monogamy doesn't have to mean monotony, but if you settle into a routine too quickly, it might.

When you do something out of the ordinary with someone—when you're surprised, when you laugh, when you learn and get engaged—your body releases dopamine and norepinephrine, chemicals that bond you to the person you're with. In other words, great dates lead to actual chemistry.

That butterflies-in-stomach feeling doesn't have to end! You can still experience it six months, six years, six decades in. Just continue to make romance a priority, to make your time together special. Continue to ask your boyfriend out on dates.

HOWABOUTWE COUPLES

If you need some date ideas, or just motivation to get out of the "ordering delivery and watching *The Daily Show*" routine, may we humbly suggest HowAboutWe Couples? Here's how it works: You sign up for a membership, and for a monthly fee, we'll send you on one awesome, personalized date a month. In other words, we take care of all the annoying stuff (planning, reservations, etc.), and you get to go enjoy a one-of-a-kind night out with your significant other. Pretty sweet.

GLOSSARY

***

Cyrano *(verb)*: When you ghostwrite texts or emails for a friend who doesn't know what to say to her crush.

Date Downgrade: When someone changes date plans to something more casual, thus lessening the intensity of the date.

Dresser: A drink you have while getting ready for a date. (Something clear!)

Dropping the Girlfriend/Boyfriend Bomb: When you find a subtle (or more often not-so-subtle) way of dropping your significant other into conversation so the other person knows you aren't available/flirting.

The Fadeout: When you just sort of … stop … returning … the calls/texts … of someone with whom you've gone on a date or multiple dates.

Friendcest: When you hook up with someone your friend has already hooked up with.

Friendicator: The person you invite along to hang out with you and someone you suspect might be interested in you, in order to make clear that This Is Not a Date.

Home Game/Away Game: A home game is when you bring someone to your place. An away game is when you go to his place.

Mimbo: A male bimbo. ("They're the ones who talk about working out and act physically interested but have nothing going on above the waist." —Jaclyn, 28, Chicago)

Popcorn Flirting: Flirting that gets you nowhere, that doesn't actually lead to anything. Full of air and ultimately unsatisfying.

The Post-Hookup Summit: The conversation that needs to happen after you drunkenly hook up with an acquaintance, to determine/establish that, "Hey, we're cool."

Recycling: Hooking up with or dating someone whom you've previously hooked up with or dated.

Rounding the Bases Backward: When you hook up with someone and then start dating afterward.

Sock Gap: When guys take off everything but their socks in bed.

INDEX

CREDITS AND ACKNOWLEDGMENTS

HowAboutWe would like to thank:
Lauren Nathan, for her instrumental and tireless work on this book; Charlie Melcher, for all of his help; the Team at Harlequin, especially Deborah Brody, for seeing that *Modern Dating* needed to get out there; Paul Kepple and Ralph Geroni at Headcase Design and A.J. Garcés for lending their talents; Hanna Rosin, Katie Heaney, Leandra Medine, Claire Cavanah, and Lauren Leto for their contributions; Brooklyn Roast, for their daily coffee delivery; our Gchat buddy lists, for always being willing to answer a question or two about dating; and finally, thank you to everyone who has posted a date on HowAboutWe in the last two years, for providing both data and inspiration.

Melcher Media would like to thank:
Christopher Beha, David Brown, Susan Burke, Holly Dolce, Shannon Fanuko, Myles McDonnell, Carolyn Merriman, Gabriella Paiella, Paraag Sarva, Julia Sourikoff, Anne Torpey, and Megan Worman.

howabout*we*.com
Co-CEOs: Aaron Schildkrout &
Brian Schechter
Creative Strategist: Scott Alden
Writer: Chiara Atik
Date Report Editor: Michelle Dozois
Data Scientist: Kate Huyett
Additional Editorial Support: Erin Scottberg

Produced by

MELCHER MEDIA
124 West 13th Street
New York, NY 10011
www.melcher.com

Publisher: Charles Melcher
Associate Publisher: Bonnie Eldon
Editor in Chief: Duncan Bock
Editor and Project Manager: Lauren Nathan
Production Director: Kurt Andrews
Editorial Intern: Lynne Ciccaglione

Design by Headcase Design
www.headcasedesign.com

Illustrations by A.J. Garcés:
p. 10, pp. 14–17, p. 23, p. 30 (center), p. 37, p. 44, p. 59, pp. 62–63, p. 74, p. 76, p. 82, p. 86, p. 91–92, p. 95, p. 104, pp. 117–118, p. 120, p. 134, p. 156, p. 159, p. 164, p. 168, p. 172 (center), p. 181, pp. 184–185, p. 120, p. 156, p. 192, p. 195, p. 201, pp. 204–205, pp. 207–208

Illustrations by Headcase Design:
cover, p. 3, p. 12, p. 24, p. 30 (icons), p. 36, p. 46, p. 53, p. 61, p. 64, pp. 66–68, p. 70, p. 78, p. 81, p. 83, p. 85, p. 96, pp. 102–103, p. 106, pp. 109–111, p. 114, p. 121–122, pp. 124–125, pp. 130–133, p. 136, p. 148, p. 150–151, p. 154, p. 162, pp. 166–167, p. 170, p. 172 (icons), p. 174, p. 178, p. 182, p. 186, p. 194, p. 198, p. 202

Back flap, from top to bottom: Lisha Brown, Scout Tufankjian

Enjoy three free months
on HowAbout*We*.com

Now that you've diligently read this entire book, I can let you in on a little secret: You can't learn everything from a book, especially not dating. You can read tips and get encouragement. You can see what other people are doing on dates. You can discover some strategies that might serve you well in the future. But ultimately, dating is a skill *best learned* by going on dates.

Put the book down and go practice! You know, by now, how to get dates. (If you have a really bad short-term memory, refer to Chapters 2 and 3 for a refresher.)

To make things extra easy for you, we're offering three free months on HowAboutWe.com for everyone who buys this book. Just follow these three steps:

1. Go to HowAboutWe.com/MODERN-DATING.
2. Create a profile.
3. Enter the code below on the upgrade page.

You read this whole book; you deserve a kickass dating life. Now go get one.
—Chiara

Scratch here
for your one-time-use access code

Please note: This book cannot be returned once the sticker has been scratched off.